close-up
MAGIC

Nicholas Einhorn

Photography by John Freeman

southwater

To Hilary, Stanley and Francine
for their never-ending support,
And to my wife Joanne for the magic
she gives me every single day

This edition is published by Southwater

Southwater is an imprint of
Anness Publishing Ltd
Hermes House
88–89 Blackfriars Road, London SE1 8HA
tel. 020 7401 2077; fax 020 7633 9499
www.southwaterbooks.com; info@anness.com

© Anness Publishing Ltd 2004

UK agent: The Manning Partnership Ltd, tel. 01225 478
444; fax 01225 478 440; sales@manning-partnership.co.uk
UK distributor: Grantham Book Services Ltd, tel. 01476
541080; fax 01476 541061; orders@gbs.tbs-ltd.co.uk
North American agent/distributor: National Book
Network, tel. 301 459 3366; fax 301 429 5746;
www.nbnbooks.com
Australian agent/distributor: Pan Macmillan Australia,
tel. 1300 135 113; fax 1300 135 103;
customer.service@macmillan.com.au
New Zealand agent/distributor: David Bateman Ltd,
tel. (09) 415 7664; fax (09) 415 8892

A CIP catalogue record for this book is available
from the British Library.

Publisher: Joanna Lorenz
Managing Editor: Judith Simons
Project Editor: Felicity Forster
Editor: Judy Cox
Photography: John Freeman, assisted by Alex Dow
Hand Model: Jennifer Schofield
Designer: Steve West
Jacket Design: Balley Design Associates
Production Controller: Darren Price

Previously published as part of a larger volume, *The Art of Magic*

10 9 8 7 6 5 4 3 2 1

The author and publishers have made every effort to ensure that
all instructions contained within this book are accurate and safe,
and cannot accept liability for any resulting injury, damage or
loss to persons or property, however it may arise. Matches and
rope should be used with caution.

contents

close-up
MAGIC

introduction

Performing close-up magic to a small group of people is not just a starting-point before you go on to better things – it can often be more impressive than big, spectacular tricks on stage. The audience, thinking they are closely watching your every move, are all the more amazed when they fail to catch you out. If you have never before had an interest in learning magic, then be warned.

Above: Close-up magic involves the use of small objects, most of which can be found around the home. There are many tricks with sugar cubes and sleight of hand, for example.

Above: A box of matches is small and can be carried easily so that you are always ready to perform a trick. Matches are ideal for creating optical illusions and simple impromptu magic.

Above: The dinner table is a good place for entertaining friends with magic. Items such as glasses, napkins and cutlery make excellent props for dinner party tricks.

You are at the beginning of a journey that could and often does last a lifetime!

I became interested in magic while watching a magician on my fourth birthday and knew at that very moment what I was going to do for the rest of my life. That was many years ago and I have been performing, creating and learning ever since.

Those of you who have already learnt a few magic tricks know how much fun it is to amaze and amuse people. Magic as a hobby is unique in that it not only fascinates the person studying it, but family and friends also. This is one reason why magic is such a wonderful pastime. Another is the sense of achievement from mastering any of the skills you undertake to learn.

Magic is also universally recognized as a wonderful form of entertainment. If you ever get the opportunity to visit one of the many magic conventions that take place all over the world, you will see a wide mixture of people. Every ethnic background is represented – young and old, amateurs and professionals, students and people in every career imaginable – but all of them share one thing in common. They all love magic.

Many of the routines and magic tricks in this book can be performed at a moment's notice with whatever objects happen to be lying around. You may want to break the ice at a meeting in the office, entertain at a dinner party or show a few tricks to your children. Whatever the situation, you will be in a position to perform something amazing.

Within this book you will find over 80 miracles to learn and perform. Many are very simple and are what magicians call "self-working tricks". Despite this term, do not expect that the tricks will work themselves. However simple a trick may appear to be, practice and rehearsal are always required to enable the performer and performance to look polished and professional. You may only wish to learn one or two of these magic tricks, but if you perform them with confidence you will be amazed at the reaction you will receive, and may well be inspired to learn more.

If you learn everything in this book, and practise the techniques until you feel comfortable using them, you will have an excellent grounding in the basics of close-up magic. If you want to learn more, you will find details of your nearest magic shop at the back of the book.

The methods for all the tricks are clearly explained, with close-up photographs showing each step. For convenience, the explanations are from a right-handed person's point of view; left-handed readers can reverse the left and right hands.

Above: Clinging Cutlery is the perfect dinner table stunt: a fork sticks to your hand, suspended without any help. Your guests will be totally mystified.

Above: The Cups and Balls is one of the most famous tricks, performed by many professional magicians. It is easy to perform and amazing to watch.

Above: The Impossible Coin Balance is a good way to win a drink at the bar, and you can challenge your friends to reproduce the effect.

Professional magicians use many of the tricks in this book, and very soon you will be performing them too. You may be surprised at just how simple some of these tricks are to perform, but do not be disappointed. The easier the method the less there is to go wrong.

Remember how you felt the first time you saw a magician make a coin or thimble vanish right before your eyes? Or that time a brightly coloured silk handkerchief was produced out of thin air? Well, in learning magic you are about to give up some of that sense of wonder in order to allow others to experience and appreciate the art. This brings us on to a very important point.

Above: There is an added dimension of fun when you invite a member of your audience to take part in a trick. Even when very close-up, your helper will not know how the trick was done.

Above: Some tricks require a little preparation in advance, for example gluing a piece of paper to a banknote. Perfect preparation is the key to these type of tricks' success.

keeping the secret

A magician's golden rule is always to keep the secret. There are several reasons for this. You are investing time and effort in learning the magic tricks in this book. When you perform them properly, the first thing people will say is "How did you do that?" which is the ultimate compliment because it means that they were amazed. Some of the tricks are very simple to perform, so you would disappoint people by letting them in on the secret. If you tell your friends how a trick works

you become nothing more than a presenter of clever puzzles and they will no longer give you the credit you deserve. If they are amazed, baffled and entertained, they will want to see you perform over and over again.

People often think the secret to a trick is very complicated and involves mirrors, wires and trapdoors. Allow their amazement to continue. To take this sense of wonder away is like telling someone how a film ends before they have watched it. Keeping the secret is also fundamental to the continuing success of magic as an art form. If everyone knew all of the secrets, then magic could eventually cease to exist.

Above: Keeping the secret is a magician's golden rule. Once you have learnt how to do a trick, never tell your audience the secret.

Learning magic has long been a "chicken-and-egg" scenario because if magicians do not tell people their secrets, how is it possible to learn? You are holding the answer in your hands. This book has been written to introduce you to the basics of the art of magic, and a little beyond. Whether you choose to continue further is entirely up to you.

You are taking the time to learn something that can make you memorable and popular for all the right reasons. If you keep the secrets, the secrets will keep you.

Above: A good presentation style is vital in the art of magic. All the best magicians put their own personality into their performances. "Magic" is always created by the magician, not the trick.

We hope that regardless of whether you learn or perform any of the magic inside this book, you will respect the art of magic by keeping the secrets to yourself.

fooling people

There is a big difference between fooling someone and making someone look a fool. Some people will feel threatened when they realize that you are going to be "doing a trick on them". They may respond with a line such as "Oh! Please don't pick on me."

They assume that you are going to make them feel silly or make them look foolish. Always be aware of this. There is a fine line between amazing someone and frustrating or offending them. The best route to success is to win your audience over by creating a rapport with them – a feeling of mutual respect. This will become second nature if you are aware of it from the outset.

"Magic" is created by the magician, not by the trick. What does this mean? Simply that a trick with a poor performance is merely a puzzle. Combine a fun presentation with a great performance and you can create miracles.

misdirection

Paris
in the
the spring

Read the sentence in the triangle. Read it again. Did you notice that the word "the" is printed twice? Chances are you did not. This is an example of how you can look directly at something and yet fail to see the whole picture.

Misdirection is a very important part of magic and is in itself a subject that could fill the whole of this book. All you need to know for now is that misdirection is the name given to the technique of directing someone's attention away from what you don't want to be seen. This may mean diverting their eyesight away from your right hand as it secretly places an object in your pocket, or making them think something is going to happen to a coin when it was the glass they should have been watching.

There is an art to making misdirection subtle and difficult to detect. When used correctly, it becomes invisible. As you work through the tricks in this book, you will be introduced to many different ways of using misdirection. When you begin to use this psychological tool with confidence, you will be amazed at how much you can get away with!

Above: Practising can sometimes be very frustrating, especially when you are attempting some of the effects that require manual dexterity. Do not give up. Just like learning to ride a bicycle, the more you practise, the better you will get.

practice, patter and style

It is vital to practise if you wish to succeed with any of the tricks in this book. The best way to learn is to read through the instructions of a trick from beginning to end and then try it out step-by-step, as shown.

Once you have learnt the order of the moves, put the book to one side and practise by talking out loud and looking at yourself performing the trick in a mirror. You may feel silly doing this initially, but a mirror is the perfect way to see what your audience will see. Often you can correct your own mistakes by following this technique.

Patter is the term used to define the words that will accompany the trick. It is a very important aspect of your overall presentation and should be considered carefully. Plan everything you will say and how you will say it, even if the words seem obvious. You will create a more polished performance by doing this. Some tricks require you to talk through what you are doing; others may need a simple story to accompany the routine. Remember to put your personality into the performance.

Think about the kind of style you wish to create. Do you want it to be fun and comical, or serious? If you make the style an extension of your personality, you will find this easier.

magic shops

There are shops dedicated to selling magic all over the world, in places you would never imagine. Have a look in your local business directory to find out where your nearest shop is located. Magic shops usually keep fairly quiet about their existence, and only a few of them advertise widely in order to stop the merely curious from learning too many secrets.

Some magic shops are like Aladdin's cave – small, dark and mysterious. Others are modern, bright and spacious. There will be experienced demonstrators behind the counter ready to show you what each trick does, and they will be able to recommend certain tricks to you, depending on your ability. As well as individual tricks, you will see magic books not to be found on the shelves of your local bookstore. Many of the books written by leading experts in the field of magic will be too advanced for a beginner, but there are others written for the aspiring amateur. Videos and DVDs are the latest way of learning magic.

You will find all of these things and more inside a magic shop. You may also be surprised at who you meet in such places. I have often bumped into famous magicians who I recognized from their performances on television.

watch and learn

Next time you watch a professional magician, even if you know the secrets of each trick, admire the performance and try to see beyond the trick in order to understand what really makes the magic work. By now you will have realized that there is far more to being a good magician than you first thought, but many of the things we have discussed will eventually become second nature.

If this book inspires and encourages you to learn more about the art of close-up magic, you will find a hobby that will fascinate you for the rest of your life. You are already on your way to learning some of the greatest secrets ever kept, and to creating moments of happiness and amazement for people everywhere. Your journey is just beginning…enjoy!

Below: The audience here is seen waiting to watch a magic show. It is often difficult for a lay person to appreciate how much time has been spent on planning and rehearsal in order to put together such a performance. In a theatre, atmospheric music and carefully designed lighting can change the mood and help to add drama to the performance. These theatrical tools are a vital ingredient for a full show of magic, where a variety of performance styles can often make the whole experience far more dynamic and therefore more enjoyable to watch.

magicians' equipment

Most of the magic tricks in this book require very little in terms of special props or equipment. Nearly all of the items needed will be found at home, and the special props that are required for certain effects can be made very easily, as will become apparent.

If you intend to perform magic seriously, however, it is advisable that you visit a local magic shop and invest in a few essential items. In a shop you will be able to talk to the experienced demonstrators behind the counter, and find out about tricks that involve the use of specially made props. Magic shops are also a good source for books, videos and DVDs about magic.

There are hundreds of magic shops all over the world that you may wish to visit in person or on the Internet; you will find some of these listed at the back of the book. If your area is not listed, take a look in your local business directory.

newspaper

newspaper and books

Two good examples of objects that you can find easily without having to go to a specialist magic shop are newspaper and books. Newspaper is used in tricks where strips are cut up and then magically restored, and books are used in mind magic, to give the impression of mind-reading.

books

close-up mat

Your first purchase might be a close-up mat. This is basically like a large computer mouse pad with a rubber base and a spongy felt top which makes spreading cards and picking up objects much easier than other surfaces such as a wooden table. Close-up mats are available in a range of different colours and sizes. Once you have a close-up mat, you can perform magic anywhere and will not have to worry about finding a nice surface on which to work. In the event that a close-up mat cannot be found, then it is advisable to work on a soft surface such as a tablecloth.

close-up mat

silks, cups and balls

Colourful silk handkerchiefs, together with attractive props such as the Cups and Balls, may be worth your serious consideration. The aluminium cups shown here are specially manufactured for this one trick, and there are many different styles and sizes available.

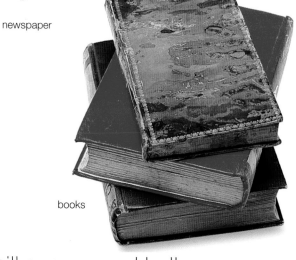

brightly coloured silks

cups and balls

rope and string

For the magic tricks in this book, most types of rope or string will suffice. If you would like a more professional rope, magic shops will be able to supply you with hanks of specially made soft "magicians' rope". This is relatively inexpensive, and available in a wide range of colours. Try to find a rope that has a high cotton content, and one that is soft and flexible.

blue and white rope
and ball of string

stationery

In order to make some of the special props, you will need a few items of stationery, such as envelopes, paper, scissors, a scalpel, pen and pencils, and adhesives. Professional equipment is always available from your local magic shop, but it is fun to make up the various props. Also, constructing props yourself can often help you to understand how they operate.

envelopes, removable sticky
notes, scissors, scalpel, pencil,
pen, glue stick, reusable adhesive
and adhesive tape

household items

General household items – such as silverware, napkins, glasses, matches, dice, thimbles and sugar cubes – are useful for many magic tricks. They are especially suited to "impromptu magic" because performances can be off-the-cuff, with little or no preparation necessary.

silverware, napkin, glass, matches,
dice, thimbles and sugar cubes

money

Banknotes and coins are props that are easy to find, and can be used for an enormous range of magic tricks. You do not need to have new banknotes – many routines require folding or even gluing them – but shiny new coins create the best impression and are easier to see than old coins.

banknotes
and coins

history of mystery

The history of magic is so long and interesting it could easily fill every page in this book. This is not intended as a definitive account but as a brief introduction to some of the most important events and names in magic's rich history, showing how they helped to move the art forward.

magic and magicians through the ages

It is difficult to pinpoint with accuracy exactly when magic began. To start with, we need to define what we mean by "magic". Man's ability to create fire could be described as a "magical" happening, but we are only concerning ourselves here with the type of magic used as a form of entertainment.

The earliest documented evidence to suggest a performance of magic was found in the Westcar Papyrus, written about 1700BC, which tells a story that goes back to about 2600BC. Dedi, an Egyptian magician, was summoned to entertain King Cheops. One of his tricks involved cutting off an animal's head and then bringing it back to life unscathed. Dedi was asked to do the trick again using a prisoner. Much to the king's disappointment, he declined to do so, but repeated the effect with an ox instead.

The Cups and Balls is often mistakenly considered to be the earliest magic trick. It features in what was once thought to be the earliest known illustration of a magical performance. Egyptologists have dated a painting on a wall at an Egyptian tomb at Beni Hasan as being between 2500BC and 2200BC. It depicts two people playing with four cups. Recently there has been much speculation whether the absence of balls in the painting nullifies the claim that it is indeed the Cups and Balls. It certainly is an ancient trick, however, and is still popular today. There are many variations, but the basic effect is that of balls magically passing from cup to cup, appearing and disappearing at the magician's

Above right: *Le Joueur de Gobelets* is an early engraving which suggests that the Cups and Balls has been a popular trick for street performers for a very long time.

Right: This late fifteenth-century painting by Hieronymus Bosch is called *The Juggler*. It is another example which highlights the popularity of the famous Cups and Balls. Magicians were often referred to as "jugglers", which explains the title of the painting. Did you notice the man in the back row stealing the purse of the person in front of him?

Above: The incredibly successful Isaac Fawkes was a regular performer at London's annual Bartholomew Fair. He is seen here producing many objects from an apparently empty bag.

Below right: John Henry Anderson became known as "The Wizard of the North". His daughter Louise accompanied him on stage.

will. The trick often finishes with the surprise production of large objects from beneath the cups – sometimes even live chicks and mice! HRH Prince Charles became a member of The Magic Circle in London in 1975 after visiting the society and performing this classic trick.

By the eighteenth century magic was a very popular form of entertainment. Isaac Fawkes (1675–1731) was responsible for generating much of the interest in Britain. He worked at large fairgrounds and gathered huge crowds for his incredible tricks, many of which relied on spectacular mechanical principles that were well ahead of their time. One of these mechanical marvels was an apple tree which blossomed and bore fruit in less than a minute. He became very famous, amassing a fortune before his death.

Giuseppe Pinetti (1750–1800), born in Italy, was another of the most important figures in the history of magic. Inspired by the success of Isaac Fawkes, he also displayed mechanical marvels. He was hugely successful wherever he appeared, and is known to have frequently performed for royalty. In 1783, while he was performing in Paris, Henri Decremps, a Parisian lawyer and amateur magician, exposed Pinetti's methods in a book. Ironically, the exposure only helped Pinetti's fame to spread, and he became even more popular. In 1784 he performed at the Haymarket Theatre in London, an important event because it marked the move of magic from the streets and fairgrounds to the theatre, inspiring a whole new generation of performers.

John Henry Anderson (1814–74) was a Scottish magician, often known as "The Wizard of the North". He was very successful throughout Europe, America and Australia and was, prior to Harry Houdini, the most successful publicist in magic. Anderson was known for his large props, which were often made of solid silver. He amassed a fortune but lost it after several theatres in which he was working burnt to the ground, leaving him bankrupt.

By now, society had recognized magic as an art form. Its popularity and success continued fruitfully into the next century as a steadily increasing number of magicians performed to larger audiences. In the days before motion pictures and television, magic was one of the most popular forms of live entertainment and performers such as those mentioned here generated enthusiastic responses wherever they performed.

magical inventors

Inventors are vital to the continuation of the art of magic and their revolutionary ideas often bring about great changes. Some inventors are also great performers, but many take a back seat and prefer to watch someone else breathe life into their creations. Here we take a look at some of the most important inventors in magic's history and those who are leading the field today.

Jean-Eugène Robert (1805–71) was born in France. He later added his wife's name to his own, becoming Robert-Houdin, and will forever be known as "The Father of Modern Magic". Robert-Houdin was a pioneer and innovator who opened his own Theatre of Magic in Paris in 1845, where he performed and thrilled audiences with his original work and amazing automata, including a version of Isaac Fawkes's tree that grew and bore fruit. He also wrote several books on magic, which were undoubtedly the best available at the time. His style and ideas were often copied by others but never equalled.

A century after Robert-Houdin's death, the French government issued a commemorative postage stamp to celebrate the life of their most famous magician.

Another French inventor was Buatier De Kolta (1847–1903). Although he performed frequently, his real strength was his ability to create and invent. He was responsible for some of the most incredible illusions of the time, some of which are still being used today. One example is the Vanishing Lady, or the

Above: Jean-Eugène Robert-Houdin was a mechanical genius and successful performer whose literary works inspired the young Harry Houdini.

Above left: This postage stamp was commissioned by the French government 100 years after Robert-Houdin's death in recognition of his achievements and as France's finest magician.

Right: Buatier De Kolta, one of magic's greatest inventors and also a fine sleight-of-hand magician. Many of his creations are used to this very day by the world's leading illusionists.

De Kolta Chair, as it is now known. A woman would sit on a chair in the centre of the stage. A sheet of newspaper was laid on the floor to show there was no trapdoor, and the woman was covered with a large cloth. As the cloth was whipped away, she vanished. This remains one of the most beautiful illusions to watch. Another of De Kolta's famous tricks was the Vanishing Bird Cage, in which a small cage containing a bird would be made to disappear without a trace. This particular trick was performed by illusionist Carl Hertz in 1921, who created a sensation when he vanished a bird cage for members of the House of Commons in England.

Servais Le Roy (1865–1953) was born in Belgium but moved to England at an early age. He was well known for his rendition of the classic Cups and Balls trick, and even more so for some of his inventions. These were revolutionary at the time, and are still used in one form or another by many large illusion acts all over the world. If one had to single out a particular illusion, it would have to be the Asrah Levitation. An assistant is covered in a thin sheet and made to levitate slowly from the ground to a position high in the air. The sheet is pulled away and the assistant melts away in mid-air.

The English magician Percy Tibbles (1881–1938) spelt his family name backwards, leaving out one "b", to become known as Selbit. He created many superb and widely used illusions. In about 1921 he performed a new invention of his that started a wave of excitement which was to spread around the globe. Sawing Through a Woman became the most famous illusion of all time. Selbit's American contemporary Horace Goldin was inspired by this illusion and quickly developed a variation called Sawing a Woman in Half. Since then, countless versions have been invented with a surprising number of different methods – with or without boxes, using large or small saws, and most recently using lasers.

Guy Jarett (1881–1972), born in Ohio, USA, was one of the most important inventors of the twentieth century. He was an odd man with many antisocial habits, but his knowledge of magic and his ability to create new and fresh methods for illusions remain unmatched. His 21-person cabinet became legendary. A small cabinet, barely large enough to hold five people, was

shown empty. Despite the cabinet being isolated in the centre of the stage and off the floor, 21 people were made to appear from within. As a special effects consultant, Jarett provided illusions for several Broadway shows and for the most popular magicians of the time, who were thankful for fresh ideas. It was his idea to make an elephant appear on stage, and a similar method was used by modern superstars Siegfried and Roy. In fact, many of today's illusions work on principles devised and developed by this genius in magic.

Robert Harbin (1910–78) was born Ned Williams in South Africa. He moved to England and created a huge impact with his numerous inventions. Harbin is perhaps best known for the incredible Zig-Zag Girl illusion. An assistant stands inside a small cabinet, which is then divided into three sections by two large, imposing blades. The middle section of the box is pushed over to one side, creating a sight that simply defies explanation. This is still one of the most popular illusions among performing magicians. Harbin was also a busy cabaret performer, working on cruise ships all over the world and at private events in London hotels.

Magicians today are as inventive as ever. Pat Page, Ali Bongo, Jim Steinmeyer, John Gaughan, Paul Osborne, Tommy Wonder, Juan Tamariz, Eugene Burger, Max Maven, Paul Harris and Michael Ammar are just a few of those who have helped to move the art of magic forward thanks to their incredible knowledge and sheer originality.

Left: Robert Harbin presenting his most famous illusion, the Zig-Zag Girl. It was to become one of the most popular and most performed illusions of all time. The original cabinet is currently on display at The Magic Circle Museum, London.

literary experts

Until the relatively recent introduction of videos and DVDs, magicians relied heavily on books for information about the art of magic. The first English book to include magic was published in 1584 and since then tens of thousands of books have been written covering every aspect of this ancient art. A plethora of new material continues to appear at an almost daunting rate, but a few literary works stand out as being particularly important to magicians of their time and to today's students and performers.

During the sixteenth and seventeenth centuries people who performed magic were often feared to be working in league with the Devil. As history books tell us, witchcraft was heavily frowned upon and was considered a crime punishable by death. In 1584 Reginald Scot published *The Discoverie of Witchcraft*, the first English book to expose the methods of magicians and to reveal how they used sleight of hand rather than evil powers to perform their magic. The book even contained the method used for decapitating animals as performed in Egypt by Dedi in about 2600BC. It caused huge controversy, and King James I ordered it to be publicly destroyed.

In the same year, 1584, a less well-known French book was published – *Clever and Pleasant Inventions* by J. Prevost. Unlike *The Discoverie of Witchcraft*, this book completely focused on the performance of magic as entertainment rather than denouncing witchcraft.

Above right: This diagram, taken from Reginald Scot's *The Discoverie of Witchcraft*, clearly shows the workings of a decapitation illusion. When the trick was performed, a curtain would cover the trestlework to hide the secret. It is just one of the many illusions exposed within this famous book.
Right: The original title page of Reginald Scot's book, which was fiercely condemned during the reign of King James I.

Between 1876 and 1911 Professor Louis Hoffmann (1839–1919) wrote numerous books. These included *Modern Magic*, *More Magic* and *Later Magic*, as well as English translations of earlier books by Robert-Houdin. It is said that Hoffmann's books have had more influence on the art of magic than any others. They revealed many secrets and were responsible for a whole new wave of magicians. His English translation of the *Memoirs of Robert-Houdin* captured the imagination of a young man who was later to become the most famous magician of all time and whose name is synonymous with magic – Harry Houdini.

S.W. Erdnase wrote *The Expert at the Card Table*, published in 1902. This exposed the underhand methods of card cheats and introduced many of the sleight-of-hand techniques that today's card sleights are based on. His name spelt backwards is E.S. Andrews but the true identity of Erdnase still remains a mystery.

In 1910 the French magician J.B. Bobo wrote *Modern Coin Magic*, which is still regarded as one of the best reference books concerning this branch of the

Ricky Jay and Edwin A. Dawes, together with the late Milbourne Christopher and Walter B. Gibson, are all recognized for their important literary works which unveil many interesting and significant facts about magic's history. These names represent some of the leading experts in the field of magic history. Gibson was also known for having written a vast number of magic books for the amateur.

Many other magicians have written books and essays discussing the psychology of magic and "misdirection". They include Dariel Fitzkee, Eugene Burger, Tommy Wonder, Michael Ammar and Darwin Ortiz. With the exception of Fitzkee, who died in 1977, they continue to be major authorities in magic.

Today there is a steady stream of new magic books being published. Most of these can only be bought at magic shops and will not be found on the shelves of your local bookstore. Reading the ideas, philosophy and psychology of respected magicians is a rewarding experience, and a great opportunity to increase your knowledge and develop your skills.

Left: British-born Professor Louis Hoffmann wrote many books on the subject of magic, several of which became legendary.

Below: Harlan Tarbell was thought by many to be the most influential writer on the subject of magic after Professor Hoffmann. His huge *Course in Magic* continues to be recognized as one of the finest sets of books available.

art. The American Harlan Tarbell (1890–1960) was the author of *The Tarbell Course in Magic*. Originally designed as individual lessons which were sent regularly to subscribers, they were eventually bound in six volumes. The contents form one of the most comprehensive references to magical effects and methods, and include every type of magic imaginable. This huge set of books is highly regarded among professionals and amateurs alike. After Tarbell's death more volumes were added, and there are now eight volumes in total.

In 1949 Jean Hugard and Frederick Braue published *The Royal Road to Card Magic*. This book teaches a huge range of card techniques and an array of card tricks that would be received as well now as when they were written. It was considered to be the foremost book on basic card magic, though it has now been superseded by the work of the Swiss, Roberto Giobbi. Giobbi expertly documented advances in modern card handling in a later set of books, *Card College Volumes 1–4*, published from 1998 onwards.

magical venues

In 1873 the Egyptian Hall in London was the venue for regular performances by John Nevil Maskelyne (1839–1917) and George Alfred Cooke (1825–1905). These performers were known for their ability to weave their magic into short plays, which gave their tricks and illusions meaning and helped to provide a context for the magic. This clever concept can be seen in the work of some of today's great illusionists such as David Copperfield, who brings together music, dance, theatre and magic to incredible effect.

Maskelyne and Cooke's original show was due to last for three months, but Maskelyne went on to become a regular fixture at the Egyptian Hall for some 30 years, during which time he became part manager. Many of the world's great magicians had performed at this venue before him, but during this period it became synonymous with magic. He would invite singers, pianists and jugglers as well as other magicians to perform, thus making every show unique and therefore watchable over and over again. The Egyptian Hall became known as "England's Home of Mystery". It closed in 1905 but Maskelyne's success enabled him to buy a new theatre in which to continue his shows. St George's Hall, only a few minutes away from the old site, became "The New Home of Mystery". Shortly after the new venue opened, Cooke died and Maskelyne found a new partner, David Devant (1868–1941). Devant was considered one of the best magicians of the time and the duo became an even more successful team than Maskelyne and Cooke. After Maskelyne's death the theatre remained a magical showcase for the greatest performers of the day. St George's Hall was finally sold in 1933. It is now a hotel.

In 1905 a group of 23 magicians decided to start a magic club in London. The Magic Circle is now one of the world's most exclusive and famous magic societies. Early meetings took place in a room above St George's Hall, with David Devant as the society's first president. Its Latin motto "Indocilis Privata Loqui" roughly translates as "Not apt to disclose secrets", and any member who breaks this rule stands to lose their membership.

Above: The Egyptian Hall in London was originally a museum. It was built in 1812 and later became known as "England's Home of Mystery" when Maskelyne and Cooke became regular performers. It was a popular venue for many of the leading magicians of the time, until its demolition in 1905.

Left: The enchanting and awe-inspiring spiral staircase at The Centre for the Magic Arts, London. This is The Magic Circle headquarters, one of the most prestigious magic societies in the world. It houses a library, museum and theatre.

In 1998 The Magic Circle bought an old office block near London's Euston Station and transformed it into The Centre for the Magic Arts. Meetings are held every Monday evening, and the facilities include a library which boasts Europe's largest collection of books on the subject and a museum that houses some of the most important artefacts in magical history. The theatre is used regularly and often features shows that are open to the general public.

In 1963 the Academy of Magical Arts was established in Hollywood by William Larsen Snr. The Magic Castle, erected as its headquarters, is possibly the foremost magic building in the world today. It remains a private members' club and showcases leading magicians from around the world, who perform nightly. Soon after its opening, the Magic Castle became a mecca of magic and many of the great magicians relocated just to be near this home of mystery. More than a few of today's magic stars owe a great deal to the Larsen family, who continue to run this incredible club and to promote the good name of magic.

comedy magicians

Arthur Carlton Philps (1881–1942), known simply as Carlton, performed mostly in London's music halls in the early 1900s. He developed a unique style which made him a hit with his audiences. Carlton was incredibly skinny and his skin-tight black tights made him look even thinner; he also wore a bald wig and increased his height with platform shoes. He was known as the "Human Matchstick" and later as the "Human Hairpin". His very presence on stage was enough to set the audience laughing, and his comical throwaway lines made him into a commercial act that would be received as well in today's theatres as then. When the music halls began to close during the late 1930s and trade became slack, Carlton put on a lot of weight, which destroyed the very thing that made him so funny. Sadly his final years contained little to laugh about and he died having lost everything he once had.

Tommy Cooper (1922–84) was without doubt one of England's funniest men. After discovering early on in his career that his audiences found him more entertaining when he made mistakes, he created a character that will never be forgotten. Like Carlton before him, Cooper could make an audience howl with laughter without saying a word. The fact that he was a big, tall man with a face made for comedy probably helped. Always wearing his trademark fez, Cooper was a superb comedian who wrote some of the funniest lines and sketches, for example:

I went to the dentist. He said, "Say aaah."
I said, "Why?" He said, "My dog died!"

On 15 April 1984 Cooper collapsed on stage at Her Majesty's Theatre, London, and soon afterwards he died of a massive heart attack. The show was being broadcast live to viewers all over Britain. Most of the audience thought it was part of an elaborate joke and bellowed with laughter until the curtain dropped and it became clear something was very wrong. It was perhaps how he would have liked to have died – in front of his adoring fans. Britain, however, had lost an incredible comedian and magician.

American comedy magician Carl Ballantine (born 1922) became a well-known actor and magician throughout the United States after television catapulted his name across the nation in the 1950s. "The Great Ballantine", as he is known, performed on many of the top shows of the time including "The Ed Sullivan Show", "The Steve Allen Show" and "The Johnny Carson Show". Like Tommy Cooper, Ballantine realized early on in

his career that his magic and style was best suited to comedy, and his act is a catalogue of disasters from start to finish. His superb timing and hysterical sight gags have made him a legend among comedy magicians.

The well-known American duo Penn and Teller (born 1955 and 1948 respectively) have been together since 1975. After ten years performing on and off Broadway, they shot to fame following many television appearances. They became known within the industry as "the bad boys of magic" due to their offbeat brand of humour and their apparent exposure of magical methods. Although their style would not be to everyone's taste, they have extended the boundaries of magic and comedy, and their numerous television specials have won several industry awards. Penn and Teller's busy schedule of live shows continues to amaze and amuse huge audiences wherever they perform.

Above: Tommy Cooper was one of Britain's funniest magicians and best-loved comedians. His trademark fez and recognizable laugh, together with many hysterical routines and sketches, left his audiences bellowing with laughter.

close-up magicians

The tricks you will learn in this book belong to the category known as close-up magic. Compared to the other areas of the art, this is a fairly recent branch of magic which has become hugely popular and has seen a sharp increase in bookings for magicians at private parties, banquets and corporate events. Its popularity among magicians is probably due to the fact that expensive props are not necessary and there is no need for a stage or particular lighting. The beauty of close-up is that it can be performed anywhere and with virtually anything.

Nate Leipzig (1873–1939) was a Swedish-born magician who moved to America and became an important authority in close-up magic. Perhaps best known for tearing up a cigarette paper and restoring it in a very magical way, his techniques and effects are still studied today and remain in constant use.

The great Max Malini (1873–1942) was of Polish-Austrian descent but moved to America at a young age, where he became a wonderful performer of intimate magic. He was also very highly paid for his larger shows and became famous throughout the world during the 1920s when he gave many prestigious performances for royalty and heads of state. His astounding magic is still talked about and there is much to be learnt from his methods and philosophy. There is more information about Malini and his magic in the introduction to the chapter on Dinner Table Magic.

Fred Kaps (1926–80) was an outstanding Dutch magician who became famous within the magic fraternity in the 1950s. He was a role model for many future magicians – his skill and style were impeccable and his ability to change his performance to suit his audience was outstanding. As well as performing wonderful close-up magic, Kaps was known as a superb manipulator with a great sense of humour. His incredible sleight of hand ensured a faultless act that was enjoyed by millions of people all over the world.

Canadian Dai Vernon (1894–1992), famous for his rendition of the Cups and Balls, was a legend of magic affectionately known among his peers as "The Professor". He was quite simply regarded

Above: The great Max Malini performed for some of the most important people of his time. Several US Presidents, as well as royalty throughout Europe, enjoyed his magic. Many of Malini's tricks are still talked about, and even today one wonders how he could make such large objects appear from under his hat without anyone seeing how it was done.

as the absolute master. His close-up magic, at which he excelled, was of a quality rarely seen, and it is doubtful whether the close-up magic of today would be where it is without this wonderfully talented man, whose influence on magicians everywhere was substantial. Another of the most influential magicians of the twentieth century was Tony Slydini (1901–91). Originally from Italy, Slydini lived in New York and was the East Coast's answer to Vernon. Magicians would travel from all over the world to see him and to persuade him to teach them his techniques for "misdirection", which are still largely recognized and used to this day.

Right: Dai Vernon was the leading authority on magic and misdirection. He was and still is known with affection as "The Professor". He was also a highly skilled and very successful silhouette cutter, and in his early years made a living by cutting people's silhouettes at fairgrounds in and around New York.

Far right: "The Professor" was particularly known for his beautiful rendition of the classic Chinese Linking Rings. This fascinating effect is still being performed frequently by magicians, and many of the techniques that Vernon developed are now recognized as standard "moves".

American Albert Goshman (1920–91) should be noted for two reasons. He was an exceptional performer who understood "misdirection" in a way very few people do. To watch a performance of his legendary coin under the salt shaker routine was an unforgettable experience. Despite two people watching as closely as they could, Goshman made coins continually vanish and reappear under the salt shakers, which were right in front of the spectators. He also built a factory which manufactured sponge balls for magicians. Sponge balls have become incredibly popular because of the interest they generate with audiences, and more importantly because of their ease of manipulation. The development of sponge-ball magic owes a great deal to Albert Goshman, but sadly it is believed that constant exposure to the fumes of the factory contributed to his death.

Today the field of close-up magic is led by the likes of Eugene Burger, Paul Harris, Juan Tamariz, Michael Close, Guy Hollingworth, Lennart Green, Daryl Martinez, David Williamson, Michael Ammar, Tommy Wonder, Ricky Jay, John Carney, Harry Lorayne and many more wonderful performers.

Left: Nate Leipzig, a true master of sleight of hand, travelled the world with his act. Leipzig would perform only for a small crowd he had invited upon the stage. The reactions of this lucky few were apparently enough to delight the rest of the audience – only a true showman could manage that.

illusionists

As well as illusionists such as De Kolta, Selbit and Servais Le Roy, there are others who were known predominantly for their incredible showmanship and dramatic presentations.

Born in France, Alexander Herrmann (1844–96) was the youngest of 16 children. His father Samuel and his brother Compers were both magicians, and by the time Alexander decided to build a career in magic, his brother Compers was already known as one of the best magicians of the day. However, the style Alexander adopted was well ahead of his time. Instead of the usual presentations associated with magicians, he injected a great deal of humour and fun into his shows. He quickly became the foremost magician of the mid- to late nineteenth century. "Herrmann the Great", as he became known, worked extensively in America, and later in England he performed large illusions regularly at the Egyptian Hall. By the time of his death he was so famous that he was regarded as a living legend.

The American Harry Kellar (1849–1922) belonged to the same era as Herrmann, and there was a bitter rivalry between them. Kellar filled the gap in the market after Herrmann died, touring his show all over the world. He was heavily influenced by England's master magician Maskelyne, and tried to purchase the method and rights to perform Maskelyne's levitation illusion. Maskelyne declined to sell, but this was the first of many effects to appear suddenly in Kellar's repertoire with remarkable similarities to Maskelyne's creations. After Kellar's retirement in 1908, he announced Howard Thurston as his successor. Thus Howard

Above: Alexander Herrmann had a huge family and a background steeped in entertainment. He was the most famous of the Herrmanns, and created a sensation with his act. He toured successfully around the globe, often performing for royalty.

Above: Harry Kellar was regarded by many as America's leading magician. He toured his illusion show all over the world.

Right: Howard Thurston's impressive illusion show assured him of rapid success.

Thurston (1869–1936) became America's leading magician. He updated Kellar's show and added fresh illusions, including the vanish of a motor car. He was a huge success, and his repertoire became so extensive that it took ten railway carriages to transport all of the necessary props and scenery.

William Ellsworth Robinson (1861–1918) was born in New York. After a fairly uneventful beginning to his magical career he decided to create a Chinese act, influenced by the famous Chinese magician of the time, Ching Ling Foo. Robinson chose the "oriental" name Hop Sing Loo but soon changed it to Chung Ling Soo, the name that was to make him famous. Soo's act was as colourful and visual as it was entertaining, and proved very successful with his audiences. He made bowls full of goldfish materialize from nowhere and caused money to appear in abundance. Although he was considered a competent illusionist, it is not this for which he is famous. The one trick that will forever be associated with Chung Ling Soo is the notorious Bullet Catch. A bullet is marked for later identification and shot from a gun aimed at the magician. The marked bullet is, incredibly, caught before it has a chance to do any harm and the markings are verified. On 23 March 1918 at the Wood Green Empire in London, Chung Ling Soo was shot on stage after the gun misfired. He was rushed to hospital but died the following

Above: A poster depicting Chung Ling Soo performing the famous Bullet Catch which finally killed him after the gun misfired.

morning. He was not the first magician to lose his life performing the Bullet Catch, but he was certainly the most famous.

German-born Sigmund Neuberger (1872–1911), later known as "The Great Lafayette", was a superb and very dramatic performer who worked all over the world. He was famous for incorporating large animals into his illusions. The scale of these shows had never been seen before and he was one of the highest-paid performers. Beauty, one of the dogs he used in his act, was a gift from Houdini. Lafayette's love for his animals, especially Beauty, was obsessive and frequently mocked. He died on 4 May 1911 when the Edinburgh theatre he was performing in burnt to the ground during a performance.

Horace Goldin (1873–1939) was born Hyman Goldstein in Poland. He moved to America in his teens and became known as "The Whirlwind Illusionist" because of the speed at which he rushed through his repertoire. Goldin's most famous illusion was Sawing a Lady in Half. In his first version, his assistant was placed inside a box which was then sawn in half and split down the middle before being reassembled. In 1931 he presented a new version which disposed of the boxes and gave the audience a clear view of a huge circular saw ripping through the lady's midriff. The publicity generated by this spectacular illusion was incredible, and Goldin travelled the world with his show. He died suddenly after a performance at the Wood Green Empire in London, on the same stage where 21 years earlier Chung Ling Soo had been shot dead during his bullet-catching routine.

Above: The Great Lafayette, one of the highest-paid performers of his time, with his beloved dog Beauty, a gift from his friend Harry Houdini.

Bess, tied and bound. It was, as you can imagine, a staggering illusion and one that has stood the test of time. Modern versions of it are still performed frequently by many of today's illusionists. One particular act, The Pendragons, are able to effect the change faster than anyone else in the world, in under half a second!

Before long Houdini was known specifically for his escapology, and often offered large monetary rewards to anyone who could produce a pair of cuffs from which he could not escape. His escapes from milk cans, safes and prison cells excited, amazed and thrilled audiences the world over. Another of his most famous illusions was the Chinese Water Torture Cell, in which he was shackled and placed upside down inside a tall glass-walled cabinet filled with water. Despite the impossibility of the situation, Houdini was able to escape from the confines of the tiny cabinet. The publicity he generated was huge, and he sustained a continued and successful performing career until 22 October 1926. One of his incredible abilities was to withstand punches to the stomach without discomfort, but on this occasion he was struck without warning and suffered a ruptured appendix. Houdini bravely continued his engagements until he could no longer stand the pain. Peritonitis had set in and a week after being punched, at the age of 52, one of the greatest showmen on earth passed away. In death he became even more famous.

Harry Houdini (1874–1926) was born Ehrich Weiss in Budapest. Soon after his birth the Weiss family moved to Appleton, Wisconsin, USA, and it was here during his teens that Ehrich developed a keen interest in magic after reading the *Memoirs of Robert-Houdin*. Adding an "i" to the end of this great magician's name, he changed his name to become Houdini. He married Wilhelmina Beatrice Rahner, known to all as Bess, and together they toured Europe with an act that quickly established Houdini as a sensation wherever he went. One of the illusions most associated with Houdini is Metamorphosis. Houdini would be handcuffed and tied up inside a sack, then placed in a large trunk which was locked shut. A curtain would be pulled around the trunk and Bess would tell everyone to watch carefully as she entered the curtained enclosure. Within seconds the curtains would open and Houdini would be seen standing free of the shackles, ropes and cuffs that had bound him only moments earlier. The trunk was unlocked, the sack opened and there inside would be

Above left: An early Houdini poster showing the master escapologist bound by chains. He was possibly the greatest publicist in the history of magic. Almost a century after his death, he remains famous all over the world.
Right: Harry Blackstone Snr was a popular illusionist whose name became synonymous with magic throughout the USA during his lifetime and continued to remain known as a result of the highly successful career of his son, Harry Blackstone Jnr.

In 1918 Henri Boughton (1885–1965) changed his name to Harry Blackstone. He was America's next greatest illusionist after Thurston. As his show grew so did his repertoire, which included the incredible vanish of a horse and Sawing a Lady in Half with a huge circular saw (similar to Goldin). He was also a master of more intimate magic, which he would perform in front of the stage curtains while the next big illusion was being set up. Two of the smaller illusions associated with him were the Dancing Handkerchief, in which a borrowed handkerchief was caused to come to life, bouncing, squiggling, squirming and floating across the stage before being handed back to its startled owner, and the vanish of a canary from a bird cage held by several children from the audience.

The name Blackstone continued to be associated with magic for many years thanks to his son, Harry Blackstone Jnr (1934–97). Harry toured a smaller show in the 1960s and 70s before reproducing his father's show with some new illusions and touring it across America. He became a prominent magician on American television and a well-known and respected celebrity. He is remembered for his incredible Floating Light Bulb, which glowed, levitated and floated across the stage before sailing out just above the heads of the audience.

Few dispute the assertion that American Channing Pollock (born 1926) was one of the greatest manipulators of the mid-1900s. This suave, handsome man handled cards, coins, billiard balls and doves with a style and panache never seen before. His incredible production of doves started a whole line of copycat acts, but although many magicians strive to reach the standard of Pollock's dove productions, few succeed. It is Channing Pollock we have to thank for one of today's top manipulators and illusionists. Lance Burton (born 1960) was inspired by the work of Pollock, and is one of the few magicians who have managed to equal his incredible skill. Burton's shows in the theatre built especially for him at the Monte Carlo in Las Vegas continue to astound audiences twice daily. His repertoire includes a version of the act that won him the FISM Grand Prix in 1982. FISM is the biggest and most important magic convention in the world and the enormous competition held every three years is the Olympics of magic. Burton's illusion show enables a modern audience to appreciate what audiences in the days of Thurston, Kellar, Goldin and Blackstone Snr must have felt. He is one of the leading showmen of magic today.

Siegfried and Roy (born 1939 and 1944 respectively) were perhaps the most successful megastars and illusionists in the history of magic. Their incredible show was the main attraction at the Mirage, one of the biggest hotels in Las Vegas, and their performances were always sold out. At one time it was the most expensive show ever to be produced, with a cast of hundreds. The two German-born magicians met in the early 1960s and worked on cruise ships around the world before landing their very own show in Vegas in the mid-70s. Their sensational illusions used large white tigers and there was no shortage of lions, elephants, cheetahs and other exotic animals, which were made to appear and vanish close to and often directly above the audience. Siegfried and Roy were one of the highest-paid acts in the world, but their show closed in 2003 when Roy Horn was attacked on-stage by a white tiger.

television magicians

David Nixon (1919–78) became Britain's first regular television magician. He was a kind, gentle and popular man whose weekly show made him famous throughout Britain from the 1950s to the 70s. Meanwhile, across the Atlantic the American Mark Wilson (born 1929) also became a television legend. His show "The Magic World of Allakazam" featured many top magicians, and ensured a future of stardom and fame which continues to this day.

Doug Henning (1947–2000) was born in Canada and became a magical superstar of the 1970s and 80s. Having studied under the greatest (Dai Vernon and Slydini), he developed several stage shows that changed the face of magic with a style never before seen. He did not look like the typical magician; in fact he looked as if he had just stepped out of the 60s in full Woodstock regalia, including tie-dyed tops and flared trousers. His journey in magic began to take off when he appeared in the 1974 Broadway show "The Magic Man" and he followed this debut with eight television specials which were, and still are, among the greatest shows ever caught on camera. The fact that the shows were filmed live is testimony to Henning

Above right: Master illusionist David Copperfield, whose television specials and live shows make him one of the world's best-paid and most recognized modern-day magicians.

Below: David Nixon became Britain's first successful resident television magician. His show "It's Magic" featured many top magical acts from around the world.

and his team's incredible skill. Doug Henning became a sensation in America, touring with an awesome illusion show until he decided to leave his life of showbiz to live in India, where his religious studies became the focus of his life. He had begun work on designing a transcendental meditation theme park in Ontario, but sadly died before his dream could be realized.

David Copperfield (born 1956) was born David Seth Kotkin in New Jersey. After developing an interest in magic at the age of ten, he knew there was only one thing he ever wanted to do. He started his career on stage in the Chicago version of "The Magic Man" and was soon signed up for his own television special, the first of many which catapulted him to fame. His sensational style and incredible stage presence, together with his groundbreaking illusions, keep audiences on the edge of their seats. He is one of the world's highest-paid entertainers and also one of the busiest, performing over 500 shows a year. Copperfield made a name for himself by performing illusions that captured the world's imagination. In 1981 he vanished a Lear jet and two years later he caused the Statue of Liberty to disappear. This illusion was the biggest ever performed at the time and attracted huge television audiences, causing a worldwide sensation. These grand-scale illusions became a necessity to Copperfield's television specials and fans were eager to see what he would do next. Among other stunts, he walked through the Great Wall of China and levitated and vanished an Orient Express railway carriage. David Copperfield has become one of the most important icons in magic and will always be regarded as a leader in the field.

Paul Daniels (born 1938) became Britain's most famous magician shortly after he hit the television screen in 1970. His cheeky banter was a huge contrast to the style of David Nixon, and his catchphrase "You'll like it, not a lot but you'll like it!" was an instant success with the public. In 1979 he appeared in the Royal Variety Show and his weekly television slot "The Paul Daniels Magic Show" pulled in huge viewing figures for over ten years, winning many industry awards including the Golden Rose of Montreux. He later married his long-term assistant Debbie McGee and the husband-and-wife team became a celebrity couple recognized all over Britain. Daniels was without doubt one of the most talented magicians of the late twentieth century and a major influence on British magic.

Although not publicly famous worldwide, Luis de Matos of Portugal, Juan Tamariz of Spain and Silvan of Italy are all superb magicians, well known in their own countries for their television shows. De Matos is a suave and elegant performer of close-up magic and larger illusions, often creating mini-playlets complete with incredibly designed sets comparable in style to David Copperfield's. Tamariz is one of the most talented card magicians in the world today. His regular television shows are popular with his audiences, who recognize him as one of Spain's top television personalities. Silvan, like Luis de Matos, is an all-rounder, performing huge illusions as well as incredible close-up magic.

David Blaine (born 1973) represents a new wave of magicians. Breaking with tradition, he successfully stripped magic of its glamour and pretentiousness,

showing the world that magicians do not need a stage with trapdoors, expensive sets and careful lighting to perform miracles. Blaine takes his magic on to the streets and performs for unsuspecting members of the public. The television crew captures the surprise and awe of his spectators, and this unique approach has made him immensely successful in a relatively short time. He is currently creating the kind of publicity and awareness that has not been seen since the likes of Houdini. Blaine is known around the world thanks to the power of international media and repeats of his television specials, which are aired frequently across the globe. He is known for his ability to read people's minds, for levitating himself off the ground and for publicity stunts such as being buried alive for five days, standing in a block of ice for over 60 hours, standing on top of a pole for 35 hours and starving himself inside a suspended perspex box for 44 days. One thing is certain – his image is fresh and his style unique. Trends in magic will change, and another star will one day take the world by storm, but for now David Blaine is one of the most talked-about magicians of our time.

Above left: Paul Daniels is one of Britain's most successful television magicians, and was undoubtedly responsible for inspiring a whole new generation of conjurors during the 1980s and 90s.

Below: American street magician David Blaine stood inside a block of ice for over 60 hours as one of his feats of endurance.

dinner table magic

The dinner table is an ideal place to perform magic for your friends and family. If you take the time to learn a few clever routines, you will be able to entertain and astound people at any time. Most of these tricks can be performed without any set-up, and the items you require can be found at the restaurant or dinner table.

introduction

Glasses, napkins, cutlery, straws, cups and sugar cubes are just some of the objects often found on tables at meal times. It is a good idea to learn some magic tricks with these items so that whenever you dine with other people you are in a position to entertain. An ordinary dinner party can become a very memorable occasion with an impromptu performance, and if your guests do not know each other magic is an ideal icebreaker. You can be sure that your performance will lead to conversation and no doubt speculation as to how you achieved your miracles.

One magician known for his love of intimate performances was Max Malini. Born Max Breit in 1873 on the borders of Poland and Austria, he was taken at an early age to live in New York. Between then and his death in 1942, Malini made a name for himself in many countries around the world. While other magicians were busy performing in theatres and music halls, Malini would work for small intimate groups, often at top hotels, and for the most distinguished dignitaries of the time – including royalty and numerous world leaders. One feat of magic that will always be associated with his name is the production of a huge block of coal or ice from under his hat. His table guests, who had been in his company for several hours, were understandably astounded by the sudden production of the block, and in the case of the ice were most curious as to how such an item could be stored and hidden without melting! However, if he deemed the time and mood to be wrong, he would sometimes decide not to perform at all, despite having prepared for the trick hours in advance.

Another great story is that of Malini bending, ripping and soiling an old playing card that he would then throw face down in the gutter. Later that day, while walking with a friend, Malini would boast about his ability to name any playing card just from looking at its back. His friend might then spot the dirty card in the gutter and challenge Malini to name it. Such elaborate preparation may seem like a lot of work considering the friend might not have spotted the card in the gutter, but this kind of magic and the response it

Below: *L'Escamoteur, sur le Boulevard, Près le Chateau d'Eau* is a late nineteenth-century engraving which shows a street magician in mid-performance of one of the greatest tricks of all time – the legendary Cups and Balls.

receives is what reputations were, and still are, made on. Using Malini's philosophy, why not practise and prepare the Torn and Restored Napkin trick for your next dinner party? Wait for the right time in the evening to perform it, and cause a sensation. After dinner is usually a good time to perform because people are generally relaxed by the time they have finished their meal. If you are hosting the dinner yourself, there is no reason why you could not ensure the correct items were conveniently nearby for when you needed them.

Explained in the following pages are several effects which can be strung together (for example, Sugar Rush and Sugar Rush Uncovered). This allows you to make your performance short or long depending on how responsive your audience is. Bouncing Bread Roll and

Above left: Max Malini, the early twentieth-century conjuror, caused a sensation whenever and wherever he performed.

Top: This fork seems to be defying gravity. Or is it? Find out in Clinging Cutlery.

Above: A typical dinner table setting. Most of the items seen here – a glass, knives and forks, a napkin, a salt shaker and a pepper grinder – can be used to perform magic.

both versions of Bending Knife are quick, off-the-cuff stunts, while Vanishing Glass, All Sugared Up and The Cups and Balls are longer routines which can form part of a small, impromptu after-dinner show.

rolling straw

A straw is set on the table in front of you, and you then rub a fingertip against your sleeve. As you hold your finger above the straw, it rolls forward as if repelled by a magnetic force. The best kind of straw to use is one of the type that are supplied free in fast food restaurants. As will become apparent when you read through the method to this trick, it may be a good idea to fail a few times before finally succeeding. Your audience will become accustomed to watching you rub your finger on your sleeve and this will provide you with perfect misdirection. If a drinking straw is not available, this quick stunt will work just as well with a cigarette.

1 Place a straw in front of you on the table and rub your first finger on your sleeve. Explain that you are generating static electricity.

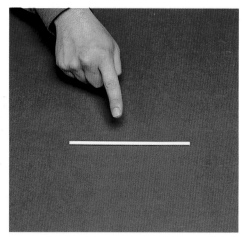

2 Hold your finger directly above the straw.

3 Move your finger forward and, as you do so, secretly blow at the table in front of the straw. The breeze will cause the straw to roll forward. Try not to change the shape of your face as you blow; all eyes should be on your finger.

clinging cutlery

This is a perfect dinner table stunt. It is easy to perform, yet completely mystifying. A fork is made to cling to the outstretched palm of your hand. The secret is explained, but moments later it transpires that you were not being entirely honest, as the fork is once again made to cling to your hand in an even more amazing fashion! The set-up takes just a few seconds.

secret view

1 Hold a fork in your closed left fist. Grip your left wrist with your right hand and open the left fingers wide. The right first finger secretly stretches out to hold the fork in place.

2 From the front, it looks as if the fork is stuck to your hand. You can stop the illusion here, but you can also go a step further. Turn your hands around, exposing the method to the trick. Return to the same position.

3 The right hand is now removed completely, yet the fork still stays suspended from the left hand. How?

secret view

4 This exposed view shows how a knife is held under your watchstrap from the outset. When you pretend to reveal your secret, the knife is covered by your first finger (see step 1).

bending knife (version 1)

A knife is held between the fingertips and gently shaken up and down. The metal seems to turn to rubber and the illusion is created of the knife bending. This illusion also works with rulers, nails, pens and many other objects. It is the perfect effect to show just before the even more impressive Bending Knife (Version 2), described next.

This optical illusion dates back a long way and is a good example of "retention of vision", which is the term used to describe the effect whereby an image remains in view a few milliseconds after it has been moved away.

At about chest level, hold a knife loosely by one end, between the thumb and first finger of the right hand. Quickly and continuously move your right hand up and down about 10cm (4in). As the knife begins to shake, it appears to become wobbly, as if made of rubber.

bending knife (version 2)

This is a great follow-up to Version 1. A knife is bent in half at right angles, then straightened out again. The optical illusion is perfect.

It is not necessary to use a coin, as seen below, because the trick works almost as well without it, but the coin does give conviction to the illusion.

secret view

1 Hold a knife in the right hand with the tip against the table. The fourth finger should rest behind the handle and the other fingers in front. Hold a coin at the top of the knife between the finger and thumb. Only the tip of the coin is seen, and it is mistaken by the observer for the top of the knife.

2 The left hand closes around the right hand as shown. The knife is supported entirely by the right hand. The left hand simply helps to hide the method.

3 The knife is pushed against the table and although the hands stay straight, the knife is allowed to fall flat pivoting between the right third and fourth fingers, as seen in this exposed view.

4 From the front, with both hands covering the method, this is how the illusion looks. Finish by raising the hands, therefore straightening the knife and showing that it has unbent itself.

bouncing bread roll

A bread roll is picked up off the table and apparently bounced on the floor, like a tennis ball. It shoots up into the air and you catch it as if it was the most natural thing in the world. This trick would work equally well with a piece of fruit such as an apple or orange, and even a pool ball at a pool table! As long as you use an object that would not ordinarily bounce, the effect will register well.

1 This trick is easiest to do sitting at a table, although once you understand the principle you can also do it standing. Hold a bread roll in your right hand, at about shoulder height.

2 Bring your hand down below the table's edge, exactly as if you were about to bounce the roll on to the floor.

3 As soon as your hand passes the edge of the table it will be out of sight. This is where you have to work with split-second timing if the illusion is to be a success. Notice how the foot is ready to tap against the floor, simulating the sound of the roll hitting the ground.

4 The moment the hand is below the table's edge, it turns at the wrist and flicks the roll up into the air as straight as possible. There should be no movement from the arm itself; only the wrist should move. A split second before you toss the roll, tap your foot on the ground.

5 Follow the movement of the roll with your head. The combination of sounds and visuals will provide the perfect illusion of the bread roll bouncing.

vanishing glass

In this amazing impromptu trick a coin is covered with a glass, which in turn is covered with a paper napkin. While the audience's attention is focused on the coin, the glass is somehow caused to disappear. You can also make it pass straight through the top of the table.

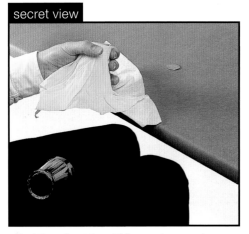

secret view

1 Perform this sitting at a table. Place a coin on the table in front of you, then place a glass, mouth down, on top of it. Cover the glass with a paper napkin from the top downwards so that the paper is stretched around the top and sides and would hold its shape even if the glass were removed; the bottom should remain open. Ask a spectator if the coin on the table is heads up or tails up.

2 Lift the covered glass up and back towards the edge of the table with one hand, exposing the coin. Bring attention to the coin by pointing to it with the other hand. This is simply misdirection to divert the attention of the spectators away from what happens next.

3 The glass should be resting on the edge of the table in front of you. Allow it to slip out of the napkin and safely on to your lap. There is no "move" as such – simply lift the glass away from the coin and allow it to fall silently. The napkin will hold its shape so a casual glance should not arouse any suspicion.

4 Carefully place the napkin shell back over the coin and remove your hand.

5 Tell the audience to watch as you proceed to smash the "glass" flat to the table under your hand. This sudden noise will create the moment of impact you should strive for. One moment the glass is there, the next it has completely disappeared!

tip *As a variation, ask the spectator to hold their hand out just above the "glass". Place your hand above theirs and bring your hand down on to theirs as the paper is flattened. This directly involves the spectator, who is expecting to feel the glass. Instead of creating the illusion of the glass disappearing, you can also finish by telling the audience that the glass went straight through the table. Simply produce the glass from beneath. If a glass is not to hand, you can do the same trick with a salt shaker or pepper grinder.*

torn and restored napkin

A paper napkin is torn into small pieces and squeezed between the hands. The pieces magically weld themselves together again. The napkins in the photographs are shown in different colours for ease of explanation.

A little experimentation with napkins will reveal that the paper is easy to tear in one direction because of the direction of the grain. Try to orientate the napkins correctly when you set up this trick so that the tearing is made easier for you.

1 To prepare, apply a small amount of glue to the top right corner of a paper napkin (at the point here marked "X").

2 Glue a second napkin to the first at this point. Wait for the glue to dry.

3 Scrunch up the top napkin into a ball. Neatness is not important.

4 Continue to squeeze the ball, making it as small as possible. You are now ready to start performing the trick.

secret view

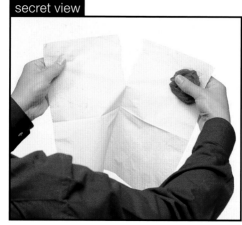

5 Hold the flat napkin in both hands so that the duplicate ball is at the top right corner on your side of the paper. Begin to tear the napkin in half down the centre.

6 From the front, the duplicate ball is hidden completely and must remain so. The napkin provides lots of cover.

secret view

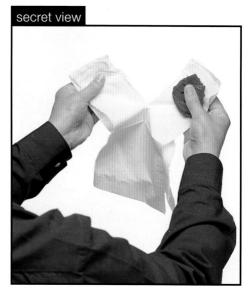

7 Place the left half of the napkin in front of the right half. Tear the paper down the centre as before.

secret view

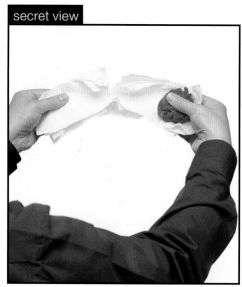

8 Place the left pieces in front of the right, then turn the strip sideways so that you can tear the strip down the centre.

9 Place the left pieces in front of the right again, then make one final tear down the centre.

10 Place the final pieces of paper in front of the right-hand pieces as before and squeeze the edges together.

11 While you are squeezing the napkins, secretly turn them over so that the duplicate napkin is facing the front. As the real napkins are the same colour, this move will be invisible.

12 Start to open out the napkin along the top edge, smoothing out the wrinkles as you go.

13 Continue to straighten it out until the entire napkin is revealed to be restored.

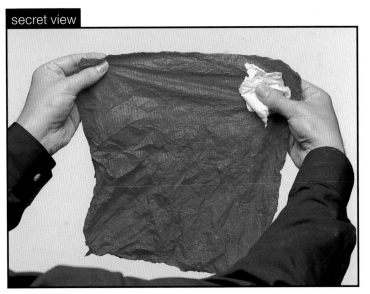

14 The torn pieces are safely hidden behind the duplicate napkin at the top right corner. To finish, crumple all the paper into a ball and discard it.

sugar rush

This is a very popular effect in magic which is also known as "Matrix". Four sugar cubes are set out in a square formation. Two playing cards are shown and used to cover the cubes briefly. The sugar cubes jump about, seemingly of their own free will, until they all meet in one corner. This is similar to the next routine, Sugar Rush

Uncovered, but it does not require difficult sleight of hand because of the extra cover created by the two cards. If no playing cards are available, you could also perform the trick using coasters or even menus – whatever is to hand. If you learn both routines, you will have a nice set piece to perform at a dinner table.

1 Set out four sugar cubes in a square formation. The cubes should be about 30cm (12in) away from each other.

2 Grip an extra sugar cube between your second and third fingers, as shown. In performance, there will always be a card on top of your fingers so this cube will remain hidden.

3 Hold a playing card in each hand, so that they both look the same and the extra sugar cube cannot be seen. Cover both the upper right and left cubes.

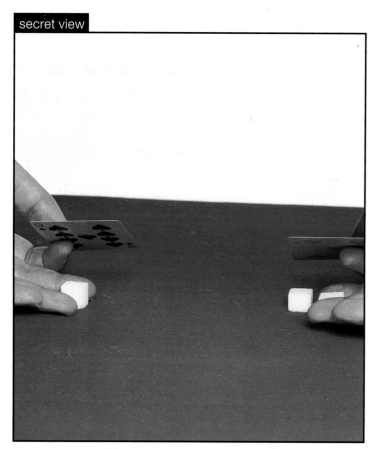

secret view

4 This exposed view shows how the right hand is about to let go of the hidden sugar cube while the left hand is getting ready to take a cube away under the card.

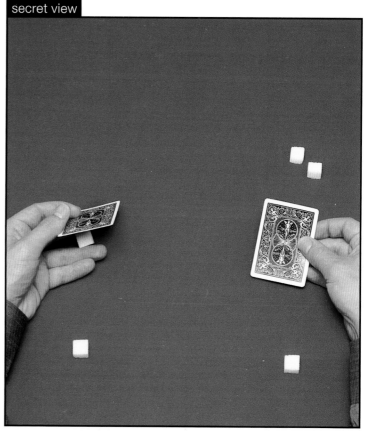

secret view

5 Move both cards to show that one cube has supposedly jumped. (Be careful not to expose the hidden sugar cube.)

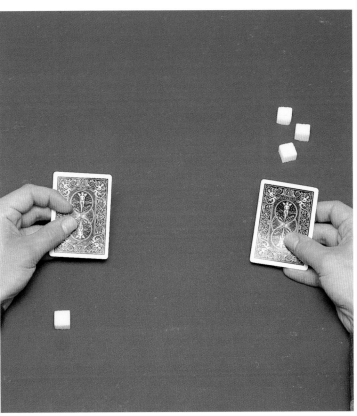

6 Cover the upper right and the lower right cubes, repeating the same move as before. Both hands should move together and at a constant pace.

7 Move the hands back to show that a second cube has moved across to join the others. Do not pause for long, but continue to move your hands to the next position.

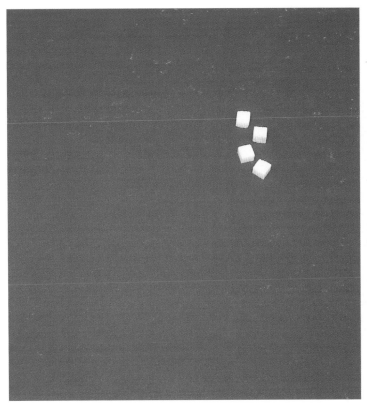

8 Cover the upper right and lower left corners, in preparation for the final sugar cube to travel.

9 Repeat the move one last time and show that all the sugar cubes are together at the top right corner.

sugar rush uncovered

Four sugar cubes are placed in a square formation on the table. The hands cover the cubes for the briefest of moments and they start to jump from corner to corner until all four cubes join together in one corner. This routine is a perfect follow-up to Sugar Rush. The order of moves is basically the same, but instead of using cards as cover, this *version relies entirely on a convincing Classic Palm. Palming a sugar cube is as easy as palming gets, which is why they are ideal for this trick. You could also use upturned bottle tops, which are equally easy to palm because of their shape and easy-to-grip edges. In order to achieve success with this effect, some dedicated practice is required.*

`secret view`

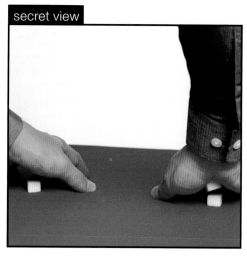
`secret view`

1 For this trick you will need a bowl of sugar cubes. Take five cubes from the bowl, secretly palming one in the right hand (*see* Money Magic chapter for a description of the Classic Palm technique). Set the bowl off to your left-hand side and set out the remaining four cubes in a square formation in front of you.

2 Cover the furthest two cubes with your hands. As you will notice, the sequence of moves is similar to that of Sugar Rush, so once you are familiar with that trick this one will be easier to learn.

3 Drop the palmed cube in your right hand and palm the one under your left hand. This should take no more than a second, and both moves must happen simultaneously. With practice, you will be able to palm and drop the cubes without any noticeable movement from the back of your hand.

4 Move both hands away to reveal that one of the cubes appears to have jumped.

5 Without hesitation, cover the top right corner with your left hand and the bottom right corner with your right hand. Do the same move again, dropping the left-hand cube and picking up the cube at the lower right in a right-hand Classic Palm.

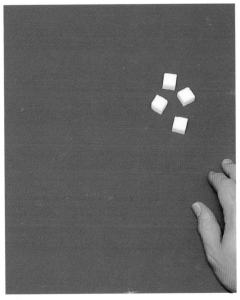

6 Move your hands to show that the second cube has moved.

7 Finally, cover the top right corner with your right hand and the bottom left corner with your left hand.

8 Perform the move one more time to show that all cubes are now at the top right corner.

secret view

9 You will finish with a sugar cube palmed in the left hand. This is easy to get rid of. Simply pick up the sugar bowl to your left-hand side and, as you lift the bowl up, allow the cube to fall in, along with the other cubes.

10 Pick up the remaining cubes on the table and openly drop them back into the sugar bowl. The great thing about this routine is that you finish completely "clean"; that is, you destroy the evidence of the extra cube when you drop it back into the bowl.

all sugared up

A number is chosen at random and written on the side of a sugar cube. The cube is then dissolved in a glass of water and the written image is made to appear on the palm of the person who chose the

number. You will need to use a very soft pencil and a sugar cube that is smooth on all sides. This routine will cause massive reactions because the effect actually happens in the spectator's hands.

secret view

1 Before you begin the trick, secretly dip your right second finger into a glass of water to moisten it. If the liquid is cold, you may be able to moisten your finger by touching the condensation on the outside of the glass. Either way, you must ensure there is some moisture on your fingertip.

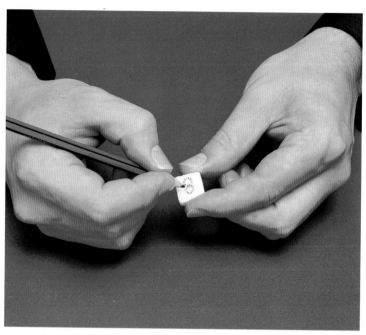

2 Ask a spectator to choose a number. Using a pencil, clearly print the number on one side of a sugar cube.

3 Squeeze the cube between your right thumb and second finger as your left hand moves the glass into view. The written number should be pressed against the moist second finger. Drop the cube into the water.

secret view

4 You have secretly transferred the graphite in the pencil to your fingertip. Now you must secretly transfer this to the palm of the person who chose the number.

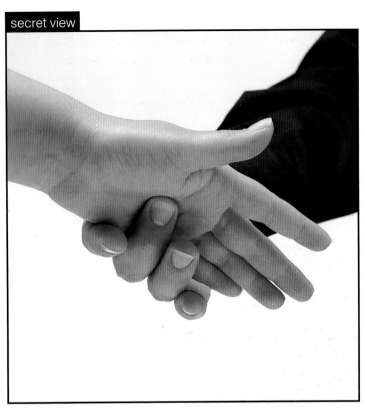

5 Ask them to hold out their hand, then take hold of it and move it to a position above the glass. As you do so, lightly press your second finger against their palm.

6 This will transfer the image without their knowledge. The spectator should not notice because you are touching them for a reason, that is, under the pretence of repositioning their hand.

7 Ask the spectator to move their hand up and down above the glass. Explain what is going to happen: "As the sugar cube dissolves, the graphite will float to the surface of the water and the heat of your hand will cause the particles of graphite to turn into a vapour which will rise from the glass and attach itself to the palm of your hand."

8 Ask the spectator to turn their hand palm up and they will see the duplication of their number, drawn on the sugar cube moments before.

knife and paper trick

Paper spots are stuck to the blade of a knife on both sides. The spots are removed, but reappear at the magician's command. The sleight taught here has been used by magicians for decades and is still *popular today. It includes the Paddle Move, which involves showing the same surface of an object twice while the spectator thinks they are seeing two different sides. This move has many applications.*

1 Tear off six tiny pieces of paper from the corner of a paper napkin.

2 Dip the tip of your finger into a glass of water, then touch the blade of the knife to transfer the spot of liquid.

3 Repeat this at two more points on the knife, then place a paper spot on each wet point – the water makes them stick.

4 To practise the sleight you will use throughout this trick, hold the knife between your fingers and thumb with the blade pointing downwards. The paper should be on the top side of the blade.

5 Twist your wrist towards you so that the knife turns over and the blank side can be shown to the spectator.

6 Twist your wrist back again, reversing the action of step 5.

7 Repeat this wrist action once more but, as your wrist turns over, push the handle of the knife with your thumb so that the knife turns over at the same time as your hand. This time the spots will appear to be on the back of the knife as well. This is the Paddle Move. Turn your wrist back again, using the Paddle Move to flip the knife over at the same time.

8 To proceed with the trick, after step 3 add three more pieces of paper to the blank side of the knife. This completes the preparation.

9 Now that you are familiar with the Paddle Move, you are ready to learn the sequence of moves for the routine. Display the knife in the right fingertips as shown.

10 Twist the wrist (without performing the Paddle Move) and show three spots of paper on the other side of the knife blade.

11 Bring the knife back to the start position and pull off the lowest spot. Pretend to slide off the spot on the underside of the knife at the same time.

12 Perform the Paddle Move, which allows you to show that the spot on the underside has also apparently been taken.

13 Repeat these moves with the second spot, in fact only taking the spot off the top of the knife.

14 Execute the Paddle Move again to show that both spots have supposedly been taken.

15 Repeat once more for the last spot remaining on the knife.

16 Using the Paddle Move, show that both sides of the knife are now blank.

17 With a shake of the wrist, quickly twist the knife between your fingers and thumb to make all three spots reappear. These can be shown to be apparently on both sides, using the Paddle Move one last time. Finish by removing the three spots, thus destroying the evidence.

the cups and balls

It has been said that a magician's abilities can be measured by the performance of this great trick, of which there are many versions. Some use just one cup, others two or three, but the effect is always similar. A number of small balls are caused to vanish, penetrate and reappear under the cup or cups, often changing into fruit and even live mice and chicks along the way! This basic version uses three balls and three cups. It is easy to perform and amazing to watch. Professional sets of the cups and balls are available from magic shops.

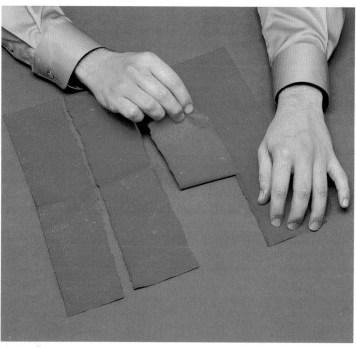

1 You will require four small ball-like objects. You can use sugar cubes for an impromptu performance, or you can fashion balls from a paper napkin torn into four strips.

2 Roll each strip into a ball. Although you will be using four balls, the audience will only ever be aware of three of them.

3 Stack three cups together, secreting a ball in the centre cup. Set the other three balls in a row in front of you. You are now ready to perform the incredible Cups and Balls.

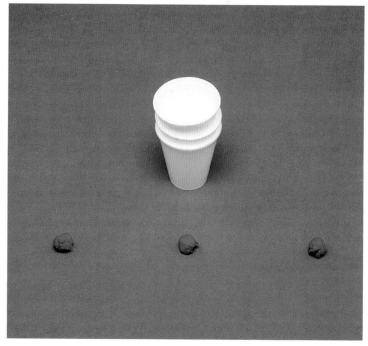

4 This shows the preparation completed and is how the cups should be set before you begin the routine.

5 Pick up all three cups in a stack with your left hand. The right hand takes the bottom cup from underneath and pulls it off the stack. Keep the mouth of the cup away from the spectator.

6 Turn this cup upside down next to the ball on your far right, as shown above.

7 Repeat step 6 with the second cup. Although there is a ball hidden inside this second cup, it will remain unseen and will not fall out if the cup is turned at a constant speed.

8 Place the second cup next to the centre ball, with the secret ball hidden beneath it. You must practise this until you can position the cup without fear of the extra ball falling out.

9 Finally, turn over the third cup and place it next to the ball at the far left. The extra ball is hidden under the middle cup.

10 Pick up the centre ball and place it on the base of the middle cup. ▶

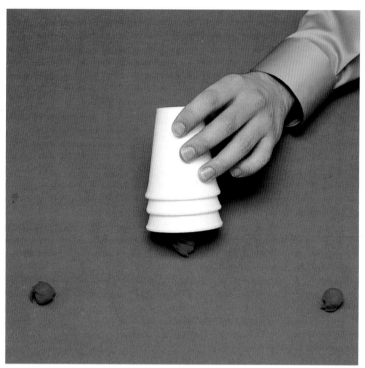

11 Stack the outer two cups on top of the centre one. Make a magcial gesture, then tilt back the stack of cups to show that the ball has apparently penetrated the centre cup and is now on the table. Pause to let this effect register with your audience.

12 Pick up the stack of cups and turn them mouth upwards again. Now repeat the set of moves and turn each cup over again. Place the first cup at the right, next to the ball. Place the second cup (containing the extra ball) over the centre ball.

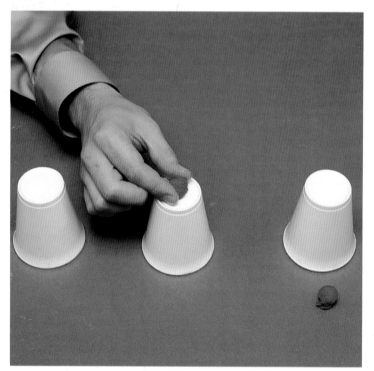

13 The third cup goes next to the ball on the left. Pick up the right ball and place it on top of the middle cup. This sequence of moves is almost identical to the sequence at the start of the routine.

14 Stack the other two cups on top as before. Make a magical gesture above the cups.

15 Tilt the cups back to show that the second ball has arrived to join the first.

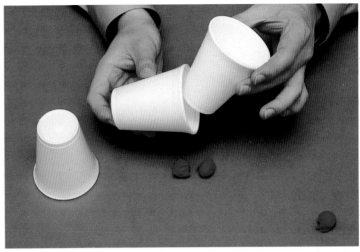

16 Repeat the moves one final time. Place the first cup to the right, the second cup over the balls already on the table, and the third cup to the left.

17 Pick up the last remaining ball and place it on the underside of the centre cup (*see* Tip for an alternative move).

18 Stack the cups one last time and make another magical gesture over them.

19 Tilt the cups back to reveal all three balls together.

20 That is the mystery of The Cups and Balls!

tip *When you reach step 17, instead of placing the final ball on the cup you can "vanish" it using a Fake Take (see Money Magic chapter) or any other technique that you are familiar with. The final ball will then be shown to have magically reappeared under the final cup.*

match
magic

Matches are a common household item and can be found almost anywhere. Their very existence is a reminder of our ability to perform real magic and create fire at will. The shape and size of ordinary matches, together with the matchbox or matchbook they are housed in, create ideal opportunities for optical illusions and simple magic tricks. With a box of matches in your pocket, you can be ready to perform an entire magic show!

introduction

One of humanity's greatest achievements was discovering how to create fire. Perhaps this was the first magic trick ever performed – it certainly must have felt like magic at the time. Our desire for "instant" fire was not satisfied until approximately 1.5 million years later, in about 1680, when a match similar to our modern ones was invented. The phosphorus used was deadly, and despite several attempts to create non-toxic alternatives, it wasn't until around 1910 that matches were made with harmless chemicals. They were then sold throughout the world. Well over 500 billion matches are now used each year – that's a lot of matches!

As a result, matches can be found everywhere. Most people have a box or two at home, and restaurants, bars and clubs will certainly have them.

> **WARNING:** Safety of yourself and others around you is the most important thing to remember when using matches. It is strongly advised that children should not play with matches, and they must be supervised by an adult if attempting any of the following tricks.

There are magicians who use fire as a major theme in their act, and build a reputation on effects of this nature. Most of the following tricks do not require you to actually light a match, so they can also be performed with cocktail sticks. As has been mentioned throughout the book, always try to be adaptable to whatever props are around you. It is advisable to learn several stunts and tricks that you can perform "impromptu" –

Above: British magician Colin Rose is well known for his fire-themed acts. One of these acts – "Fantasy in Flame" – thrilled audiences on television and in casinos and nightclubs the world over. In the 1970s his superb and dramatic manipulations of fire were enjoyed by hundreds of thousands when he toured with the legendary Richiardi Jnr.

Left: An artist's impression of the discovery of fire. Such an event would have been incredibly magical and wondrous to watch, but would probably have been met with severe apprehension.

Above: Can matches really conduct static electricity? Your friends will believe so when you show them the Static Match!

Above: The next time you need to light a candle, cigarette or cigar, magically produce a lit match from behind your lapel – Lit Match Production.

Above: A match is torn from a matchbook and lit. Seconds later it disappears, only to be found reattached inside the book – Burnt Match in Matchbook.

such tricks can often be more impressive than a fully prepared show. Performing impromptu magic should not mean that your tricks are unrehearsed; it simply means that you are able to do an off-the-cuff routine.

If you learn some of the simple stunts in the following pages, you will be able to amaze your friends by making a lit match appear before using it to light a cigarette or candle (Lit Match Production). Then you will learn how to "vanish" it using a relatively unknown method (Vanishing Match). To demonstrate the idea that wood can channel static electricity, you can make matches move and jump (Static Match and Jumping Match).

You will also learn how to make two solid matches pass through each other several times under impossible conditions (Match through Match), and how to rip a match from a matchbook, light and "vanish" it only to show the burnt match re-attached back inside the matchbook (Burnt Match in Matchbook). These are two of the best impromptu tricks in magic.

Right: Matchbox off String is the impossible penetration of one solid object through the other. The concept of penetration forms the basis for many "effects" in magic.

match through safety pin

The illusion created by this little stunt is that of a match passing through the bar of a safety pin. Although not a particularly difficult magic trick, it is a good example of how speed can deceive the eye.

It is a small party trick which can be made up quickly and cheaply with objects that most people would be able to find in their houses or place of work.

1 Using a scalpel, carefully cut the head off a match and push the sharp point of a safety pin through the centre. Close the safety pin and the set-up is completed. You may find that the match splits when you insert the pin. If this is the case, try first soaking a match for a few minutes in water in order to soften the wood.

2 Hold the safety pin with the left hand and position the match so that the top half is against the top bar of the pin. Flick the match, striking the point marked "X".

3 If you strike the match correctly, it appears as if the match passes straight through the top bar of the pin and on to the other side. In reality, what happens is that the match bounces off the top bar and rotates backwards in a complete revolution so quickly that it is virtually impossible for the human eye to see.

self-extinguishing match

You light a match and hold it in your right fingertips. You then extinguish the flame by blowing up your left sleeve! Often the best time to perform magic is when nobody is expecting anything to happen – if you catch people off guard, you can really amaze them.

Try this trick the next time you light a match. Don't call attention to your actions; just do it as if it is the most natural thing in the world. The match extinguishing itself looks very magical. Sometimes these little magic tricks can be as enjoyable as the more involved routines.

secret view

secret view

1 Strike a match and hold it up in the air away from your body.

2 Hold the match in between your right first and second fingers, so that your thumbnail is in a position to flick the match as you blow up your left sleeve.

3 Blow up your left sleeve and at the same time allow the end of the match to flick off your thumbnail.

4 The sudden movement of the match causes the flame to extinguish itself.

broken and restored match

A match is wrapped in the centre of a handkerchief. A spectator breaks the match into two pieces through the fabric, but when the match is unwrapped, it has magically restored itself. This trick is *very old, but rarely seen. It is easily prepared and simple to execute, so is ideal for those times when you are asked to perform "at the drop of a hat". It also works with cocktail sticks.*

1 Push a match into the seam of a handkerchief. The material of the handkerchief should hide the secret match perfectly – if it does not, then try using a thicker handkerchief.

2 When you are ready to perform, set the handkerchief on the table with a corner at the top and the hidden match in the corner nearest you. Openly place another match in the centre. With your right hand, bring the corner with the hidden match up into the centre.

3 Immediately fold the left corner into the middle, then the right corner, and finally the top.

4 Lift the secretly hidden match through the cloth. Hand it to a spectator and ask them to break it in half. The spectator will assume this is the same match they saw just a few moments ago.

5 Unfold the handkerchief one corner at a time. With the right hand, grip the last corner to cover the hidden match.

6 Show that the match has completely restored itself. Finish by folding up the handkerchief and pocketing the evidence of the hidden, broken match in the corner!

vanishing match

A match is held at the extreme fingertips and magically dissolved into thin air. In order to perform this amazing trick, you need to be wearing a ring on your right third finger.

This is another simple trick which is ideal for a spur-of-the-moment performance. You could also vanish a cocktail stick, but you must be careful not to stab yourself with it!

1 Hold a match between the tips of your thumb and first finger.

2 Curl your third and fourth fingers in, so that your second finger can angle the match towards the ring.

3 Use your thumb to push the match behind the back of your third finger and underneath the back of the ring.

secret view

4 This is what the move looks like from the other side. You must make sure that nobody is watching you from behind.

5 Straighten out your fingers and rub your thumb as if dissolving the match.

6 Hold your hand out flat, but with your fingers closed together.

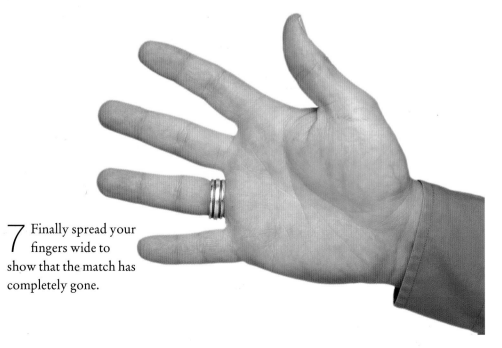

7 Finally spread your fingers wide to show that the match has completely gone.

vanishing box of matches

A box of matches is shaken and a spectator is asked to guess from the sound alone how many matches are inside. Whatever their answer, they are proven to be wrong when the box is opened and the matches have vanished! The effect of sound is strong and can be used in many different ways. For instance, once you are familiar with the workings of the principle described below, it is possible to *demonstrate a similar game to the old street swindle Three Card Monte. Three empty matchboxes are placed next to each other; one supposedly contains matches. The spectator has to keep their eye on the "full" box of matches as you move them and mix them around. You can prove that any of the boxes are empty or full at any time, depending on which hand you shake the box with.*

1 To prepare, half fill a matchbox with matches and close the box. Do not overfill the box, otherwise the sound the matches make when shaken will become muffled.

2 Put a rubber band on your left forearm, under your shirt sleeve. Place the box under the rubber band. You are now ready to perform the trick.

3 Shake an empty matchbox with your left hand. The rattling sound that is emitted comes from the hidden box up your sleeve. Ask the spectator to guess how many matches are inside the box. It doesn't really matter what their answer is.

4 Open the box and show that it is completely empty. You can hand it out for examination and allow your spectator to dismantle it if you wish.

static match

This is similar to the Jumping Match which follows, but is slightly easier to perform. One match is balanced on the edge of a matchbox and the other match rubbed against your arm to create "static electricity". As the two match heads touch, the "static" is transferred and the match on the box shoots off like a rocket. In fact static has nothing to do with the method but it makes an interesting presentation.

1 Remove one match from a matchbox. Stand the matchbox on its side and carefully balance the match on top at right angles, as shown here.

2 Rub the second match on your sleeve, supposedly to generate static electricity. Rub your foot on the floor at the same time, as if trying to harness as much electricity as possible. Hold the match between your thumb, first and second fingers. Its tip should sit under the second finger's nail.

3 Slowly approach the balanced match until the heads touch each other. You should act as if you might be about to receive an electric shock so that your actions interest the spectator.

4 As soon as the heads touch, allow the match to snap out from behind your fingernail. The force of the resulting jerk will be transferred through the first match and into the second. The second match will fly away at speed.

jumping match

Two matches are held at the extreme fingertips. One is rubbed on the sleeve and is held underneath the other. A few seconds later one of the matches flies away as if charged with electricity. The secret to the trick is the vibrations that are caused by rubbing a match against your fingernail. These vibrations make the match jump. They travel along one match and through the other, making it move without any apparent cause. If you practise enough, you can make the match jump completely off your finger and on to the table.

This effect will also work with toothpicks and even chopsticks. Try linking this trick with the Static Match explained above.

1 Rub a match against your sleeve, saying that you are charging it with static electricity. Then hold its edge between your right thumb and first finger. Position your second finger so that the match is pulled against the base of the fingernail.

2 Balance the second match on the first match, using your left first finger.

3 Pull the right hand's match back against your fingernail and scrape it against the nail. This is a tiny movement, which is completely unseen. The balanced match will begin to jump as the vibrations travel along.

lit match production

The next time you need to light a cigarette or a candle, simply reach behind your lapel and produce a lit match! As with all effects using matches and fire, you must be extremely cautious.

This is not really a trick in itself, but it does provide a small, visual magical moment. It is nice to be able to make things happen magically; after all, if you are a magician it is only right that you can produce fire at will – why would a magician need a lighter or a box of matches?

1 To prepare, fold the striking panel from a matchbox in half.

2 Thread the striking panel through the bars of a safety pin, as shown above.

3 Carefully position a match with its head between the two surfaces of the striking panel.

4 Wrap a rubber band tightly around the match and panel to keep everything locked in place.

5 Attach this "gimmick" under your right lapel. You can leave it in position for as long as you like.

6 When you are ready to perform, reach behind your lapel and grip the match tightly with your right hand.

7 Quickly pull the match downwards and outwards. The match will strike against the panel and ignite as it leaves the gimmick.

match through match

The idea of one solid object passing through another is a wonderful concept. It is simple to understand and everyone knows that it is impossible. This superb effect can be performed at any time as long as you can find two matches (or toothpicks). Two solid objects are caused to pass through each other not once but twice!

Most magic tricks should never be repeated, but if you perform this one well you can repeat it many times without fear of the method being detected. You will need to practise this effect until you can perform the secret moves without thinking. Just a little practice is all it will take to become confident.

1 Break the heads off two matches and discard them. They are no longer needed.

2 Hold one match in each hand between the tips of your thumb and first finger. Your right first finger should be holding a rough, broken-off end. Squeeze it tightly so that the rough end sticks into the skin of your finger.

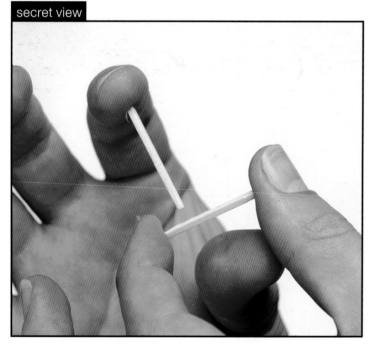

secret view

3 Tap the matches together three times. On the third tap, lower the right thumb. Because the match is wedged into your skin, it will remain suspended in the air for a fraction of a second as your thumb passes under the other match.

4 As soon as your right thumb is on the other side, re-grip the match again. The action takes place in under a second and the illusion created is of one match passing though the other. You can now reverse the above actions and remove the matches from each other. This is a great close-up magic trick.

matchbox off string

The cover of a matchbox is threaded on to a length of string. Both ends are held by a spectator and a handkerchief is placed over the centre. The magician reaches under the handkerchief and without any tearing or cutting is able to remove the box from the string.

To make the trick self-contained, find an opaque silk handkerchief that is thin enough to fold up and place inside the box together with the string. This way you can carry the whole trick around in one box.

1 Carefully prise open the glued joint of a matchbox cover, using a scalpel. Try to keep the card as flat as possible. It may take several attempts with different covers to split the box open without damaging the card.

2 Apply some reusable adhesive to a couple of points along the joint so that you can open and close the box repeatedly. When closed, the matchbox cover should look normal and arouse no suspicion. You are now ready to perform the trick.

3 Thread the matchbox cover on to a piece of string. Ask a spectator to hold one end of the string in each hand.

4 Cover the box with a handkerchief, explaining that the magic has to happen under the cover of darkness.

5 Reach under the handkerchief and unstick the prepared cover. Remove it from the string, then re-stick the join, making sure that you line up the sides of the box as evenly as possible. Display the box and remove the handkerchief. Try linking this trick with another that utilizes a piece of string, silk or a matchbox. There are many suitable effects in this book.

burnt match in matchbook

A match is torn out of a matchbook and lit. The burnt match vanishes and is found re-attached back inside the book. If you *learn this trick well, you will have a very strong piece of magic at your disposal wherever there is a book of matches around.*

1 Before you begin the performance, open a matchbook and tear out a match.

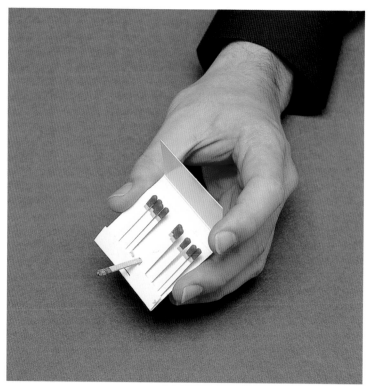

2 Bend another match forward and set it alight using the first match. Be very careful not to set alight the other matches. Blow out the flame and wait a few seconds for the match to cool.

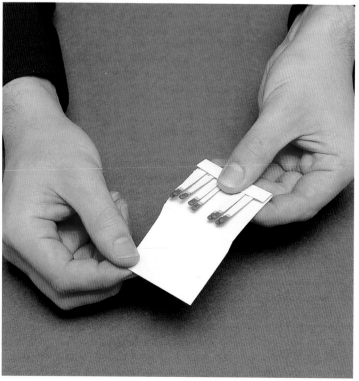

3 Hold the burnt match under your left thumb so that it is hidden from view. The preparation is now complete.

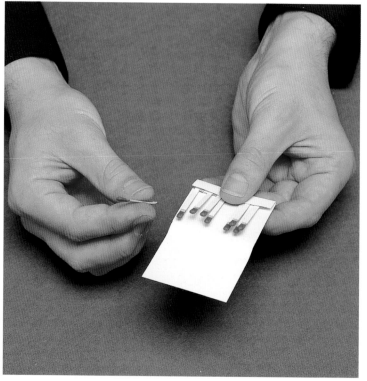

4 Show the matchbook and openly tear out one match, making sure the bent match remains hidden underneath your thumb.

5 Close the matchbook by folding it backwards in order to keep the burnt match hidden. As the cover is closed, the burnt match is unbent and goes back into position next to the others.

6 Light the torn match and place the matchbook on the table, in view. Extinguish the flame.

7 You must now "vanish" the match using any method you feel comfortable with, such as Vanishing Match or Fake Take (*see* Money Magic chapter). Another simple vanish can be accomplished while shaking the lit match to extinguish the flame. In a continuing motion, throw it over your shoulder and across the room. (Make sure the match is extinguished before you let go!) Continue to shake your hand up and down as if the match were still there. Give a few more shakes, then slow down to a halt and show that the match is gone.

8 Open the matchbook and show that the burnt match has miraculously re-attached itself inside!

string, cord and rope magic

There is a well-known saying, "Give a man enough rope and he will hang himself." There is another, less well-known saying, "Give a magician enough rope and he will show you a trick!" The following pages explain a variety of tricks using string, cord and rope. You will soon be able to cut and restore them, make them pass through human flesh and make knots mysteriously disappear at will.

introduction

One of the most famous stories in magic is that of the legendary Indian Rope Trick. There are many versions of this trick. In one version a fakir caused one end of a long piece of rope to rise slowly into the air, where it would disappear through the clouds and remain perfectly rigid. A small boy would then climb the rope until he too vanished into the mist. In a rather gruesome moment the boy would fall from the sky limb by limb. His limbs were placed inside a basket and the rope would fall to the ground. From the basket would then rise the boy, who was found to be in perfect condition. In some stories the boy was chased up the rope by the fakir, and in others the boy simply vanished when he reached the top. The variations seem to be endless.

It is hard to pinpoint exactly when this illusion first came into existence because accounts vary and most, if not all, of those who wrote these accounts did not experience the illusion first-hand. It is believed that the first reported sightings were around 1350. Centuries later, in the early 1900s, many well-known illusionists, such as Thurston, Goldin, Hertz, Kellar and Kalanag,

Above: A typical nineteenth-century depiction of a suspension/levitation which would have been performed by fakirs trying to convince the public of their special powers. Such illusions were easily duplicated by magicians of the time.
Left: This drawing of a magic trick was published in *The Discoverie of Witchcraft* (1584) and suggests that string, cord and rope have been used by conjurors for centuries.

began performing elaborate versions of the trick in theatres across the world, much to the delight of their audiences. The addition of the famous Indian Rope Trick to their repertoire and the legend that surrounded it guaranteed valuable publicity.

Even though many of the principles of rope magic are old, there are still many new techniques being developed and invented. The French magician Tabary is currently one of the freshest innovators in rope magic. His performances have astonished magicians and non-magicians across the world and won him a coveted first place at the FISM international magic convention in 1991, making him a close-up world champion.

Magic shops sell "magicians' rope" in hanks. This is relatively inexpensive and available in a wide range of colours. You can use any type of rope, but try to find one with a high cotton content which is soft and flexible. You may find the rope needs to be cored – some ropes are made up of an outer layer and an inner core. The core can often be removed by pulling it from one end. You will be left with the sleeve of soft cotton, which makes perfect rope for manipulating and cutting.

The ends of the rope may begin to fray, and there are several ways to avoid this happening. The easiest is to stitch the ends with a thread of similar colour. Alternatively you can paint clear glue on to each end to seal the ends completely.

A staple of many magicians' repertoire is the Cut and Restored Rope effect. A length of rope is cut into two – sometimes three – pieces and caused to restore itself. There are dozens of methods in existence, and several are explained in this book. With a little thought, you can link several of these routines together to create a small performance that can be used as an act on its own or as part of a larger programme.

Above right: Seen here is a demonstration of a version of the Indian Rope Trick being performed in England, 1935.

Right: A publicity poster for nineteenth- and twentieth-century magician Carl Hertz, who regularly featured a version of the Indian Rope Trick in his illusion show.

Below: A popular rope trick wherein several silk handkerchiefs magically pass through a length of rope to which they are securely tied.

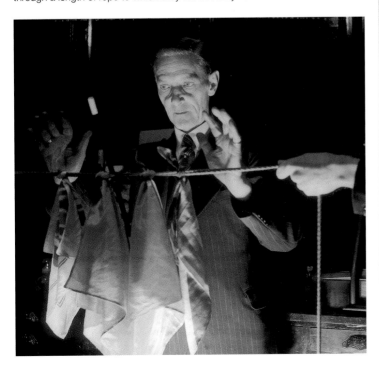

cut and re-strawed

A long piece of cord is threaded through a straw, which is then bent in half. The straw and cord are cut through the middle and displayed in two pieces, but when the cord is removed from the straw, it has magically restored itself! The best straws to use are those found in fast food restaurants. The only preparation required is a slit which must be cut and which will remain hidden by the stripes on the straw.

1 To prepare, carefully cut a slit in a drinking straw, using a scalpel. The slit should not go all the way to the ends. It is seen as a black line here for ease of explanation.

2 Hold the straw so that the slit is facing towards you and therefore hidden from anyone viewing from the front. Thread a cord through the straw so that a piece hangs from each end.

3 Hold one end of the straw in each hand and bend it in half so that the slit is on the inside.

secret view

4 Hold the straw in the left fingertips and pull the ends so that the middle of the cord slips out of the slit and behind the left first finger. Pinch the cord together with the straw between the left first finger and the thumb.

5 Cut the straw neatly in two. The middle of the cord remains hidden but the illusion created is that both the cord and the straw have been cut.

6 From the front, it can be seen that the cord is hidden behind the left forefinger, which looks very natural holding the straw in two pieces.

7 The view from your side is almost as convincing! Begin to pull one end of the cord downwards.

8 Continue pulling until the cord is removed completely. Pause to let the effect register with your audience.

9 Show that the cord is completely restored. If you wish, you can immediately hand the cord out for examination, but be sure to discard the straw in case the slit is discovered.

jumping rubber band

A rubber band is placed over the first and second fingers, then magically caused to jump to the third and fourth fingers. This is a very simple trick which you will have no trouble in mastering. You could perform this before another trick such as Linking Paper Clips.

secret view

1 Place a rubber band over the first and second fingers. The back of your hand should be towards the audience. Pull the band away from your hand.

2 Close your hand, inserting all the fingers into the rubber band. Let the band snap over the fingertips. From the front, it will simply look as though the band is on the first and second fingers.

3 Quickly open your hand. The band will automatically jump over to the third and fourth fingers.

secret view

secret view

4 It is possible to make the band jump back again. The move can also be accomplished with one hand. Hook your thumb under the band and stretch it up so that you create a gap, as before.

5 Close the fingers again, inserting them into the gap created. Release your thumb from the band.

6 Open the hand again and the band will jump back to its former position.

string through arm (version 1)

A piece of string is tied into a continuous loop. It is wrapped around a spectator's arm and magically penetrates the flesh and bone without any damage whatsoever! The principle relies on your moves being quick and smooth. The secret move is covered by the speed of the hand which, in this case, really does deceive the eye. A piece of string is a simple, compact prop to carry around.

1 Tie a piece of string, approximately 90cm (3ft) long, into a loop with a strong knot.

2 Hold the loop under a spectator's arm and ask them to create an impenetrable barrier by gripping their hands firmly together, as seen here.

3 Bring both ends of the string up to meet each other, then pass one loop through the other. Grip the string and tug it gently to show that it is unquestionably trapped on the arm.

4 Move both hands up to each other again, then hook the left first finger around the top strand of the right hand's string.

5 Maintain the first finger's grip, but release the other portion of string from the left hand.

6 Pull both hands apart until the string is held taut. It will now be above the spectator's arm. It is important that steps 4, 5 and 6 happen together in one smooth motion in order for the illusion to look its best.

string through arm (version 2)

A spectator holds out their arm and a piece of string is held underneath. A few tugs and the string passes straight through their arm to the other side! Or does it?

To prepare for this trick you need to thread two small beads on a piece of string, approximately 45cm (18in) long, tying a knot at each end. The beads should be loose and free to slide from one end to the other. These beads are not meant to be a secret but neither should you call attention to them. When you pinch your finger and thumb around them, you should hardly be able to see them. Try to ensure that the knots at the ends of the string are tied as tightly as possible so that they do not come undone while performing.

1 Starting with both beads at the left end of the string, place the string under the outstretched arm of a spectator. The string should be held taut and at the fingertips.

2 Bring both ends of the string together. Grip one of the beads tightly with your right fingers, keeping the end bead gripped in your left hand.

3 Allow the end of the string held by the right hand to drop, then quickly pull both beads taut. What really happens is that the string passes under the arm.

4 At full speed the eye cannot detect the route the string takes. The illusion of the string passing through the arm to get to the other side is very convincing!

string through ring

You can make a piece of string pass through many other solid objects. Here the same trick is performed using a spectator's finger ring.

As before, you need to attach two small beads to a piece of string. Then ask a spectator to lend you a ring. The best type of ring to use is a plain wedding band. In any event, you should avoid borrowing rings that have precious stones, in case one of them should fall out.

1 Ask a spectator to pinch a ring tightly between their finger and thumb. Thread the string through the ring. Both beads must be to the left.

2 Bring both hands together, pinching a bead between finger and thumb of each hand.

3 Drop the end held in your right hand and pull the beads apart.

4 The string appears to have melted through the band of metal. A little thought will reveal many other objects which could be used instead of a spectator's arm or a finger ring – the handle of a mug, for example.

rope through neck

The two ends of a piece of rope are seen hanging over both shoulders. Despite the fact that the rope clearly passes around the back of the head, with a sharp tug it visibly penetrates the neck. This trick also works very well with a tie, which is perhaps a more appropriate item to have hanging around your neck! Please note that care should be taken when wrapping any sort of cord around your neck.

1 To prepare, run the rope across the front of your neck, and tuck it just under the edge of your shirt collar.

2 Once this secret preparation has been accomplished, you are ready to perform. Viewed from the front, it looks as if you have a piece of rope hanging around your neck and over your shoulders.

3 Hold both ends of the rope and pull gently until the line becomes taut.

4 With one quick action, pull the rope hard with both hands. As the rope stretches out, it is pulled from under your collar so quickly that the eye will be unable to detect the secret.

impossible knot

Challenge a spectator to tie a knot in the centre of a piece of rope without letting go of the ends. Although you may find this difficult to *learn initially, once you understand which hand goes where you will be able to make the Impossible Knot in an instant, without thinking.*

1 Hold one end of a piece of rope tightly in each hand.

2 Loop the right hand over your left arm and behind the rope held in your left hand. Bring it back to a position similar to that at the start. Now move your right hand through the loop marked "X".

3 Once your hand has passed through the loop, pass it through the second loop marked "X".

4 Stretch both hands out. You should now be in this position.

5 Allow the rope to slip off your left wrist, then pull the rope taut.

6 Repeat this with the right loop. You will be left with a knot in the centre of the rope.

7 Tug both ends and the knot will disappear before your eyes!

slip knot

A knot is tied without letting go of the ends of the rope. The knot is then plucked off the rope and thrown into the audience! This is a great *"bit of business" to add to a longer rope routine because it always receives a laugh from the audience.*

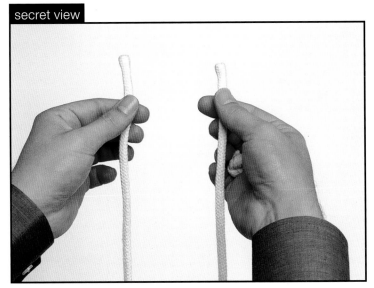

secret view

1 You will need a length of rope and a knot cut from a spare piece of rope. To prepare, hide the extra knot in your right-hand Finger Palm position (*see* Money Magic chapter). Hold one end of the main piece of rope in each hand.

2 Tie a knot without letting go of the ends of the rope, as described in Impossible Knot. Hold one end of the rope in the left hand.

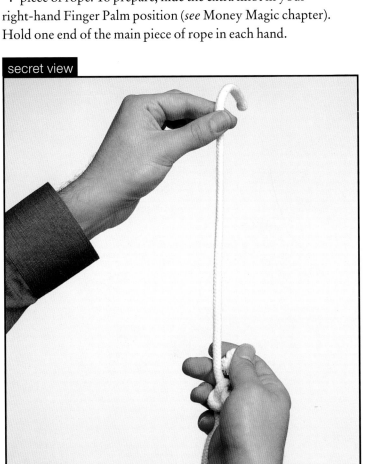

secret view

3 With the right hand, approach the knot in the rope, and with the little finger, grip the rope just under the knot. The fourth finger tugs the rope, undoing the knot as you simultaneously pluck the knot off the rope, bringing the hidden knot into view in the fingertips.

4 Viewed from the front, the illusion looks very convincing. Finish by tossing the knot high into the air and into the audience.

cut and restored rope (version 1)

A length of rope is unmistakably cut in half, yet is magically restored to its former condition. This is an absolute classic of magic and is still performed today by many magicians. You can follow this version with the next. They work perfectly together.

1 To prepare, place a pair of scissors in your right pocket. Bend an offcut of rope, approximately 10cm (4in) long, in half and hold it secretly in the left hand between the thumb and first finger. This piece must remain hidden at all times.

secret view

2 To begin your performance, hold a longer piece of rope, approximately 1.8m (6ft) long, next to the short piece, as shown. From the front, it looks as though you have only one piece of rope.

secret view

3 With the right hand, grab the centre of the rope and bring it up to the hidden short piece. It will look as though you are simply repositioning the middle of the rope so that it can be displayed. In reality you are going to switch the ropes.

secret view

4 Clip the "real" centre between your left thumb and first finger while extending the short piece up into view. The move should take seconds and should arouse no suspicion.

5 Remove the scissors from your pocket. From the front, the image is very clear. You have simply found the centre of a piece of rope and are holding it before cutting it in half.

6 Cleanly cut the rope in half. Of course you are actually cutting through the centre of the short piece.

7 Trim the ends of the rope, allowing the pieces to drop on to the floor. Continue trimming until all of the short piece of rope has been cut and dropped so that you destroy the evidence in front of the audience! Make a magical gesture, then stretch out the rope between both hands to show that it is completely restored.

cut and restored rope (version 2)

This version of this famous trick follows very well after the first. Try it out and you will fool yourself! As you will see, with the extra knot in your right hand, you can follow this with the Slip Knot trick. This *illusion works because it becomes difficult to follow exactly which section of the rope is being cut and, while it looks like the centre, it is actually a piece just a very short distance from one of the ends.*

1 Hold the centre of a piece of rope, approximately 1.5–1.8m (5–6ft) long, with your left hand and bring the right end of the rope up to meet it. With your left thumb and fingers, grip the rope about 7.5cm (3in) from the end.

2 Loop the short end of the rope away from you and over the top of the centre. Bring it back underneath, as shown. Thread the end through the gap marked "X".

3 Pull the short end of the rope and the part that emerges below the knot, to tighten the knot.

4 Cut the left-hand side of the loop just under the knot.

5 Clearly display what looks like a piece of rope cut in two and held together with a knot. Actually the rope is in one piece and the knot is simply a tiny section of rope tied around the centre.

secret view

6 Begin to wind the rope around the fingers of your left hand. As you reach the knot, allow it to slip along, hidden in the fingers of your right hand.

secret view

7 Continue to wind the rope until the knot falls off the end. Keep the knot hidden in the Finger Palm position.

8 Stretch out the rope between both hands to show that it has restored itself. You are now in a perfect position to continue with another rope trick of your choice.

rope through apple

An apple is cored and two long pieces of rope are threaded through. To further secure the apple to the ropes, a knot is made. Despite the impossibility of the situation, the apple is pulled free of the ropes without any harm to either.

This routine is ideal for a large crowd as well as a more intimate gathering. Although only small props are used, they can be made to fill a large stage with a spectator either side of you. It is an effect that, as magic advertisements would say, "Packs Flat, Plays Big".

1 Prepare two pieces of rope, each about 1.8m (6ft) long, by folding them in half. Loosely stitch the centres together. The stitches should not be too tight because they must be snapped at a later stage.

2 In performance, unfold the ropes so that they run parallel to each other. Invite two people to help you, and give them two ends each. Ask them to tug on the ropes to prove that they are exactly what they appear to be.

secret view

3 Hold on to the centre of the ropes and ask your helpers to let go. As the ends drop, grip the centre of the ropes with both hands and switch one of the ropes around, arranging them so that they are held together by the stitches. The thread is hidden from the front by your fingers, and the repositioning happens as you raise the ropes to temporarily place them over your shoulders.

4 With the ropes now safely resting around your shoulders, your hands are free to pick up an apple corer and remove the core from the apple.

5 Remove the rope from around your neck, hiding the centre in your left hand. Thread the ends of the ropes through the apple. (The two ends that go into the apple belong to the same piece of rope.)

6 The left hand provides enough cover to prevent the centre section of the rope being seen. Continue to pull the ropes through the apple until the join is hidden inside it.

7 Ask the spectators to hold the ends of the ropes. To secure the apple further, suggest tying a knot in the ropes. Take one end from each side (it doesn't matter which) and tie a simple overhand knot. Give the ends back to the spectators.

8 Cover the apple with a handkerchief, explaining that the magic has to happen under the cover of darkness!

9 Reach underneath and ask the spectators to pull the ropes taut. The thread will snap and the ropes will automatically fall away from the apple. You may find it helpful to slide the apple back and forth along the ropes as they are pulled taut.

10 Display the apple and remove the handkerchief. Give the apple to one spectator and the ropes to the other to be examined. The secret to the trick was destroyed by the spectators themselves!

mind magic

Scientists have long subscribed to the belief that humans only use a fraction of their potential brainpower. Many people believe we have, and some even claim to have, a sixth sense with which to read people's minds and make predictions about forthcoming events. Do paranormal powers really exist? People will believe they do when you show them some of the routines in this chapter.

introduction

Inspired by the performance of a fortune-telling act at the turn of the twentieth century, American-born Joseph Dunninger became one of the greatest performers of mind magic. He originally toured with a large illusion show, but soon realized the impact his mental effects were having on his audiences. Sections of his evening show became dedicated to mind magic until he decided he wanted to be known solely as a mentalist. He subsequently worked for some of the richest and most important people in America. In the early 1940s Dunninger presented a regular radio programme and continued to do so until the late 1940s, when the world of television became an attractive opportunity to spread his reputation even further. In the 1960s Kreskin, a fresh, young American mentalist, stole the limelight from Dunninger and continues to amaze both television and live audiences with his seemingly supernatural powers.

In the 1940s, on the other side of the Atlantic, British radio audiences were being mesmerized by The Piddingtons, a husband-and-wife team many people believed were truly psychic, although they themselves

Above: A publicity poster used by the successful early twentieth-century mind-reader and magician Joseph Dunninger. Take a look at the clever design of the face and you will find the eyes and nose take on a shape of their own.

Above: David Berglas became known as television's "International Man of Mystery" following the broadcast of his series throughout the UK and Europe. Performing astounding memory feats, unusual psychological experiments, manipulation and pick-pocketing, he is one of the world's most versatile magical entertainers. He is also a past president of The Magic Circle.

never claimed this to be the case. Other prominent British mentalists between the 1940s and 70s were Maurice Fogel, Chan Canasta, Al Koran and David Berglas. Berglas has only recently retired after an incredibly successful career performing magic.

In the late twentieth century American Max Maven became one of the foremost creators and performers of mental magic. Graham P. Jolley, although not so well known, is without doubt one of Britain's finest mentalists, mixing superb mental magic with rapid-fire humour and leaving audiences enthralled, entertained and utterly astounded.

None of these performers ever claimed any real psychic ability, but there is one person who does – and as a result has become a household name. Uri Geller, known predominantly for bending spoons with nothing more than his mind, also tries to convince the public of his paranormal powers by stopping watches and duplicating drawings made by volunteers – all effects which can be replicated by known magical methods. American James Randi is one of the world's leading debunkers of phoney psychics and is well known for his numerous exposures of what he believes to be Geller's methods. The famous Harry Houdini was also known for his anger against those who claimed real psychic ability. In the early 1900s he publicly challenged anyone to show him an act of

Above: Graham P. Jolley is one of Britain's funniest and most baffling mind-readers. He is billed as "The Man You Can't Keep out of your Mind" and, among other things, will make a glass shatter with mental energy, make a table levitate, and reveal the telephone numbers of names freely selected from a huge directory.

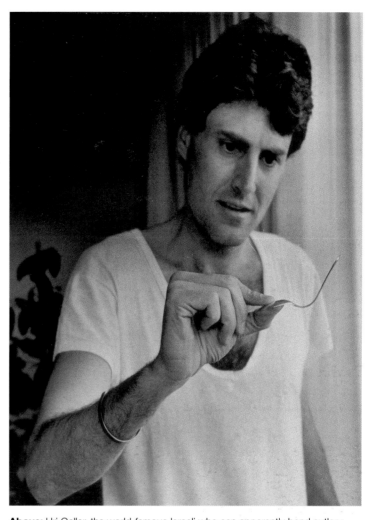

Above: Uri Geller, the world-famous Israeli who can apparently bend cutlery and other metal objects with the power of his mind. Even scientists have marvelled at his abilities, which have been studied under test conditions on a number of occasions.

Below: One of the most popular effects for a mind-reader to perform is called a Book Test. It involves a word or selection of words being chosen from a book, which are then revealed by the performer either in the form of a prediction or as a demonstration of mind-reading.

psychic power or telekinesis that he was not able to explain. Such a challenge was bold, but only helped to increase the publicity of perhaps the greatest showman and publicist the world has ever seen.

In the following pages you will learn how to create the impression of mind-reading and even of being able to predict future events. Correctly predict which of three envelopes contains a spectator's banknote (Money Miracle) or predict a word chosen at random from a book (Double Book Test). Transfer your psychic powers to a third party (Black Magic and Temple of Wisdom) and find a coin that has been secretly placed under a bottle top (Coin under Bottle Tops).

Whether you choose to perform in a serious or a more relaxed style depends on your personality, but do not be put off by the simplicity of some of the methods. Remember, the simplest tricks to perform are often the most astounding.

coin under bottle tops

A coin is placed under one of three bottle tops. The caps are rearranged while your back is turned, yet you find the coin immediately. The method to this trick relies on a short length *of thread or hair which remains unseen by the spectators. Experiment with different surfaces to work on. A tablecloth with a "busy" design would be perfect.*

1 Haberdashery shops sell a thread that is almost invisible to the human eye. You will need to find some of this "invisible thread" or use a substitute such as a hair. Attach a small piece of this thread or hair to the underside of a coin with a piece of adhesive tape. (White thread is used here for ease of explanation.)

2 It is a good idea to have this coin among others in your pocket and to casually bring it out, putting the others away. Make sure that the taped side of the coin is against the table. Place three bottle tops on the table, and ask a spectator to choose any one of them to cover the coin.

3 Ask the spectator to slide the bottle tops around while your back is turned. Explain that when you turn back you will try to divine which bottle top the coin is under.

4 When they have finished mixing the bottle tops, turn around and casually glance down in order to spot the thread. Try not to make this glance too obvious.

5 Act as though you are receiving psychic vibes, perhaps hovering your hands just above each bottle top in order to feel the heat rising from the coin. After suitable byplay, lift the appropriate bottle top to reveal the coin.

1089

A number is chosen at random and is shown to match an earlier prediction. This is an interesting mathematical principle with many uses. The number will always be 1089.

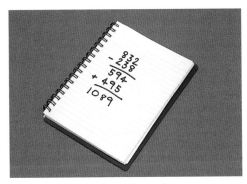

1 Ask somebody to write down any three-figure number, for example:

832

Ask them to reverse the number and to subtract the smaller number from the larger:

$$
\begin{array}{r}
8\,3\,2 \\
-\;2\,3\,8 \\
\hline
5\,9\,4
\end{array}
$$

Now ask them to reverse the total and to add both numbers together:

$$
\begin{array}{r}
8\,3\,2 \\
-\;2\,3\,8 \\
\hline
5\,9\,4 \\
+\;4\,9\,5 \\
\hline
1\,0\,8\,9
\end{array}
$$

2 Try this with various numbers. It is possible that when you reach the final stage the spectator only has a three-digit number. If so, the number will always be 198. Ask how many digits are in their final number. If they say "Three", simply add another stage. Ask them to reverse their total once again and to add them together again. This will ensure the total is 1089.

Because the number is always the same, you cannot repeat this trick to the same audience. However, you can take advantage of this knowledge, as follows.

1089 – book test

Here the distraction of the book is a smokescreen, a layer of "misdirection" designed to take the audience's attention away from the true method, which is clearly mathematical.

1 To prepare, take a book and look up page 10. Go down eight lines and look at the ninth word. Write this word on a piece of paper and seal it in an envelope.

2 At the beginning of your performance, introduce the sealed envelope containing your prediction, and ask a spectator to look after it.

3 Perform 1089 as detailed above, but do not ask the spectator to reveal the total out loud. Show your book and ask that the first two digits be used to find a page. Ask the spectator to turn to that page (page 10). The next digit, you explain, is to represent a line on that page and the final digit is to represent a word on that line. Once the word has been found, ask the spectator to read it out loud. Take back the book and have the envelope opened to show that your prediction matches the chosen word.

tip *For an extra subtlety, choose a book in which the eighth line down on page 10 does not exist. When your spectator tells you there isn't a word there, ask them to turn to the next page instead. This little hiccup makes it seem unlikely that you knew which page was going to be chosen.*

double book test

A book is chosen from a stack of books and a page and line are chosen completely at random. The magician leaves the room so it is impossible to cheat. From the chosen line, one word is decided on. The book is closed. The magician comes back into the room and, using the hidden powers of the human mind, is able to write down the word being thought of.

1 You can use as many books as you wish, but for every book you must have a duplicate copy hidden in another room. Ask a spectator to choose one of the books and note the title. Ask for a random page number to be called out, and also a line number. Then ask for a small number between 1 and 10, to indicate the word on

the line. Explain that to avoid any cheating, you will leave the room until the book has been looked at. Once the door is closed, simply look up the corresponding page, line and word in the duplicate book.

2 When you re-enter the room, act like a mind-reader and theatrically reveal the chosen word – you could write it down on a large sheet of card and ask the spectator to shout out the word first before you show your prediction.

tip *It is also possible to do this trick while remaining in the same room. You will need a friend at the back of the room. They look up the word for you and write it down on a large sheet and hold it up so that you can see it. Everyone else is looking at you, so they will not look behind them.*

just chance

This is similar to the next trick, Money Miracle, but is more suitable for a large audience or a formal show. Three envelopes are displayed on a plate and two members of the audience are given absolute freedom to choose one envelope each. The remaining envelope is left for the magician. After the choices have been made, the magician explains that before the performance a banknote was placed inside

one of the envelopes. The envelopes are opened one at a time. Each of the spectators finds a blank piece of paper inside theirs, yet when the magician's is opened a banknote is revealed.

Practise this trick in a mirror to be sure that the banknote remains hidden throughout the trick. You can also replace the plate with a newspaper or magazine.

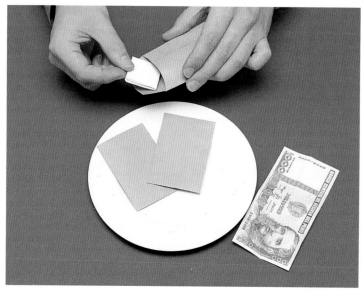

1 To prepare for this trick, you will need three pieces of blank paper the same size as a banknote. Fold the pieces of paper into eighths. Put one in each of three envelopes, sealing the flaps. Display the envelopes on a plate, flap side down.

2 Fold a banknote into eighths just as you folded the paper. Hold it in your right hand, thumb on top, fingers below.

3 Place a plate on top of the note, secretly hiding it. Before the performance, put the plate on a table with the banknote just overlapping the edge. This will enable you to lift everything at once, without suspicion.

secret view

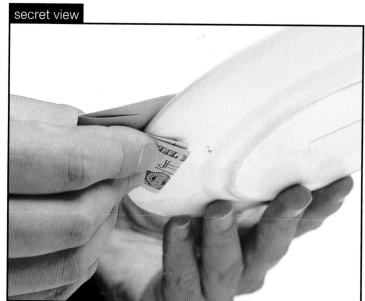

4 Explain to the audience that each of the three envelopes contains something. Offer the plate to two spectators and invite them to choose an envelope. Stress their freedom of choice. Also mention that the remaining envelope will be yours. Wait until they have removed their two envelopes. As your left hand steadies the plate, your right hand drags the remaining envelope off the plate, along with the banknote which is hidden underneath.

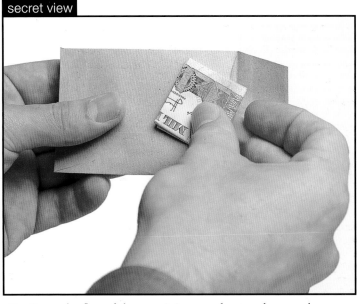

5 Orientate the remaining envelope so that the flap is towards you and the note is still hidden. Explain that before the performance you put some money into one of the envelopes and that, even though you said you would not influence the spectators, you used non-verbal communication to subconsciously direct their actions! Build up this moment so that people really do wonder if you somehow managed to make the spectators choose a particular envelope. Ask them to open their envelopes; they will find nothing but blank paper inside.

6 Open the flap of the remaining envelope and pretend to reach inside. In reality you insert your first and second fingers in the envelope while your thumb pinches the banknote on the back of the envelope. Slowly pull out the note.

7 From the front, the illusion is perfect. It looks as if the banknote was inside the envelope the whole time.

8 Finally, unfold the note and display it at your fingertips.

money miracle

Three envelopes and two pieces of blank paper are introduced. A banknote of high value is borrowed from a trusting member of the audience. The paper and the banknote are folded in an identical manner and inserted into the envelopes. While the magician's back is turned, the spectator mixes the envelopes until even they are unsure which envelope contains the note. The three envelopes are set on the table. Immediately the magician picks up two envelopes and, without

any hesitation, tears them up into shreds and tosses the pieces aside. The final envelope is opened carefully by the spectator and inside is the unharmed banknote, much to the relief of the lender!

You could use your own banknote, but one of the most important aims in magic is to make the audience care about what you are doing. If you borrow a large sum of money, there is a lot of fun to be had from this situation.

1 To prepare, secretly mark an envelope on both sides, using a pencil. The marks should be small and very light, but clear enough for you to see. (Manila envelopes often have a natural grain with an identifying feature so you may not need to make a mark at all.)

2 Fold a banknote and two pieces of blank paper in quarters. Try to make sure that all three look identical.

3 Hand the two pieces of folded paper and the banknote to a spectator and ask them to insert each one into an envelope. Be sure to hand over the secretly marked envelope and the banknote last and watch as the note is sealed inside.

4 Turn your back and have all three envelopes mixed by the spectator so that even they are not sure which one contains the banknote.

5 Ask for all three envelopes to be laid in a row on the table. The reason you marked the envelope on both sides is because you are not sure how the spectator will set the envelopes on the table, and it is better if you do not rearrange them.

6 Turn around and, without a moment's hesitation, spot the marked envelope. Slam your hands down on to the other two envelopes. Pick them up off the table and rip them to shreds. The success of this trick relies on the speed with which you make your decision. The faster you tear up the envelopes, the more amazing the finale and the more amazed your spectators will be.

7 Ask the lender of the note to carefully open the remaining envelope and remove the contents.

black magic

This is one of the few tricks for which you need a "stooge" or assistant, someone you can trust to keep the secret. The stooge is asked to leave the room (out of earshot) while a member of the audience names any object in sight. The stooge returns and the magician explains that, using the power of the human mind, he will send his thoughts across the room so that this person will be able to reveal which object was chosen. The magician points at various objects in the room – maybe ten in total – and the stooge is indeed able to choose the correct object single time.

You can repeat this trick without fear of the secret being found out if each time you change the objects and the number of things you point to.

method
The secret to Black Magic is in the title! As with many tricks, the method is very simple. Simply tell your assistant beforehand that you will point to a number of items. One of them will be black. The next object will be the chosen object. This is a very adaptable trick because you can use absolutely anything, anywhere. The stooge should act as if trying to read your mind.

Left: A number of objects, which can easily be found on a desk in an office, could be used for this trick – for example, a stapler, scissors, envelope, pen, cup and adhesive tape.

temple of wisdom

The magician explains that mind-reading requires someone to act as the sender and another to act as the receiver. A spectator is chosen to act as the receiver and leaves the room. While they are out of the room, the rest of the audience decide on a small number. Let us assume it is 12. The participant comes back into the room and places their fingertips on the temples of the magician (the sender), who pretends to send the number psychically. The receiver concentrates hard, then correctly reveals the chosen number. This can be repeated as many times as you wish.

The method relies on a "stooge" whom you have briefed before the performance and whom you can trust to keep the secret. This trick can be repeated as many times as you wish.

method
When the stooge touches your temples, pass on the chosen number by the subtle action of clenching your jaw. Your temples will pulse each time you squeeze, without anybody else noticing. Try thinking of other ways to signal the number such as the position of your feet or the number of fingers you are holding open in your lap. These subtle codes can be very baffling and are great party tricks.

silk, thimble and paper magic

Magic tricks using simple, low-cost, everyday objects such as silk handkerchiefs and paper have always been popular. Thimble manipulation is a small but very well-explored area of magic, and a thimble is an easy object to carry around. With props that are so readily available, you are able to perform at a moment's notice. The following pages introduce you to many sleights using these conveniently sized objects.

- silk magic
- thimble magic
- paper magic

introduction

Many areas within the art of magic are relatively small when compared to, for example, card tricks. However it is important to offer your audience a variety of magical effects, and so in this chapter we have grouped together three smaller areas of conjuring: magic with handkerchiefs or "silks", magic with thimbles, and magic with paper.

Handkerchiefs are frequently used in magic. Some of them are ordinary, the kind you might find in a department store, but most are extremely thin and made of silk. These can be purchased from magic shops and are ideal – they can be displayed as a large piece of fabric, but it is also possible to squash them down into a very small bundle which can be handled and hidden easily. Magicians call these handkerchiefs "silks". Silks can be purchased in a number of different sizes, the most common being 23, 30, 45, 60 and 90cm (9, 12, 18, 24 and 36in) square. They are also available in almost every colour imaginable.

The size and shape of a thimble make it a perfect object for performing sleight of hand. One of the earliest known references to thimble magic is in *The Art Of Modern Conjuring* by Professor Henry Garenne, published in 1879. The trick was entitled "The Travelling Thimble". Since then magicians have invented many ways to make thimbles multiply, change colour, penetrate handkerchiefs, appear and disappear. Many beautiful routines can be performed with thimbles, and several of the more basic sleights and tricks can be learnt in this chapter. Magicians who perform a traditional stage act often feature thimbles as part of their programme. Although small, they are visible from a distance and provide a great example of digital dexterity.

Paper comes in every shape and size and is, therefore, often an ideal medium with which to work. One of the most popular paper tricks is Torn and Restored Newspaper. A description of the effect is unnecessary as the title says it all! This chapter will reveal a simple version which allows

Above: Thimbles can be used for close-up magic or as part of a larger stage act because they can be seen for quite a distance.

Below: This wood engraving shows the early nineteenth-century French master magician Robert-Houdin producing plumes of flowers and showers of candy from a silk handkerchief.

Above: Learn The Trick Which Fooled Houdini and make a spectator's watch vanish under a silk handkerchief in impossible circumstances.

Above: Baffle your audience by magically producing a thimble from a banknote. Thimbles are wonderfully versatile objects for using in tricks.

Above: Is it really possible to move an object with the power of the human mind? Your audience will believe so when you show them the Telekinetic Paper.

you to cut a strip of newspaper into two pieces and magically join them back together again. You will also learn how to perform the classic effect, Snowstorm in China. Versions of this are still being used by many professional magicians around the world, and will finish any act in a truly spectacular fashion. Many of the tricks you will learn here can be strung together to produce a very effective act, and when you have had a little experience, you will also find that you can adapt a number of the techniques to create tricks of your own.

Below left: Snowstorm in China is a spectacular trick that makes use of – among other things – an ornamental Chinese fan and coloured tissue paper torn up to form confetti. The air is filled with a snowstorm of confetti at the end of the trick.

Below: Turn a jug of milk into a large silk handkerchief in Milk to Silk.

silk magic

There are literally thousands of tricks you can do with handkerchiefs, and some of these are described here. You should not aim to put together a whole show of handkerchief magic, as this may be a little tiresome for your audience. However, handkerchief tricks can be very spectacular, and if you use them as part of your act you can make a big impression on your audience.

simple silk production

There are dozens of ways to produce a silk from thin air. This version and the Mid-Air Silk Production which follows are two of the easiest and most magical. For extra effect, sprinkle confetti or glitter into the folds as you prepare the silk.

1 To prepare, place a silk handkerchief in front of you, completely flat and with one corner towards you.

2 Fold the silk away from you, in half and along the diagonal.

3 Begin rolling the silk from the fold. Try to make the roll as tight and neat as possible.

4 Continue rolling the silk until you reach the far corner.

5 Roll the silk from one end to the other, again trying to ensure a tight, neat roll.

6 Leave a tiny "ear" of silk at the end, as shown here.

`secret view`

7 Grip the rolled silk in the right-hand Finger Palm position (*see* Money Magic chapter) so that the "ear" of the silk is clipped tightly between your right thumb and first finger.

8 Viewed from the front, if the hand is held naturally, the silk is completely hidden. With your right hand, point to an imaginary spot in the air to your left, at about chest level.

9 Reach up to that point and simultaneously, with a gentle jerk of the right hand, let the silk unroll, ready for use in another trick.

mid-air silk production

The magician's hand is shown unmistakably empty but as they reach into the air a beautiful silk appears! Practice is required to make this *always look good, but the result is so spectacular it is well worth the effort. It makes an ideal opening trick.*

1 For this trick you must be wearing a jacket or long-sleeved shirt. To prepare, bunch up a silk handkerchief in your left hand. The bundle should be very small.

2 Extend your right arm and push the silk into the crook of your elbow, covering the silk with a fold of cloth from the sleeve.

3 Keeping the right elbow slightly bent will ensure the silk remains hidden. You are now ready to begin performing the trick.

4 Show that both hands are completely empty. Keep the arms bent just enough to prevent the silk from being exposed. (This restriction of movement is the reason why the mid-air silk production is a good trick to open with.)

5 This side view shows what happens next. The right hand quickly and sharply reaches up into the air, snapping open the fabric at the right elbow. The silk is catapulted up into the air and is caught by the right hand.

6 From the front, the silk seems to appear from nowhere!

rose to silk

A red rose worn on the magician's lapel is dramatically changed into silk. It would also be possible to add the prepared silk to a *bunch of real roses. The magician could then pluck the top of a rose off a specially prepared stem as an alternative to his lapel.*

1 You will need to wear a jacket with a buttonhole on the lapel. To prepare, lay a silk handkerchief flat, with one of the corners pointing towards you.

2 Begin rolling the silk towards the top corner. Try to make the roll as tight as possible. The neater you roll the silk, the better the rose will look.

3 Continue rolling until you reach the opposite corner.

4 At one end, bend the corner at right angles to create an "ear".

5 Starting at this end, tightly roll the silk to the opposite end. You will start to form a small bundle.

6 The finished bundle should resemble a rose. Leave a small amount of silk at the end of the roll.

7 With a match or similar object, tuck the loose end into the fold to hold the bundle in position.

8 Push the loose end all the way through to the back of the silk, being careful not to ruin the folds that make up the rose.

9 Take this loose end and push it through the buttonhole in your lapel. You are now ready to perform. At a glance, it will look just as though you are wearing a rose in your buttonhole.

10 With your left hand, hold the rose in place by gently squeezing the sides. With your right fingers, grip the centre of the rose (the "ear").

11 Gently pull the "ear" outwards, and the rose will visibly start to transform into a large silk.

12 Stretch the silk between both hands and wait for the applause! Try using some glitter or cutting up some tissue paper into small confetti-sized pieces and inserting them into the silk when you fold it. As the silk is pulled from the lapel, the contents will cascade to the floor, adding an extra magical effect.

pencil through silk

A silk handkerchief is draped over a pencil, which is pushed straight through the centre of the silk. The handkerchief is displayed to show that it is completely unharmed. This kind of impromptu magic gives you the ability to perform a miracle with objects that can be borrowed.

1 Hold a corner of a silk handkerchief in your left hand and display a pencil in your right fingertips.

2 Drape the silk over the top of the pencil so that the centre lies on the point of the pencil.

3 Close your left hand around the pencil so that the shape can clearly be seen through the fabric.

secret view

secret view

4 At the same moment, secretly bend your right hand at the wrist to bring the pencil back to a position outside the silk. From the front, this move is unseen and the silk continues to hold the shape of the pencil.

5 Immediately manoeuvre the pencil back up to a position behind the silk and under the left thumb. The moves in steps 3 and 4 are achieved in one swift motion, and should only take about one second.

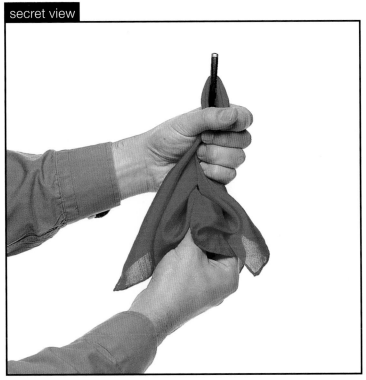

6 Give the pencil a push upwards and the tip will appear to penetrate the silk. In reality the pencil simply slides up against the silk and into view.

7 From the front, the illusion is perfect and your audience will believe the pencil has really been pushed through the middle of the silk handkerchief.

8 Pull the pencil completely free of the silk and once again display the pencil in your right fingertips.

9 Open the silk between both hands to show that it is undamaged. You can hand both the silk and the pencil to your spectators for examination, and then perhaps use the same items for your next trick.

silk vanish

A silk handkerchief is pushed into the left hand. After a suitable flourish, the hand is shown completely empty! There are many ways to "vanish" a silk. This trick uses what magicians call a "pull" – a secret holder worn out of sight, usually under a jacket. The item to be vanished is placed inside. The holder is then pulled back into the jacket by a piece of elastic. Pulls are available from magic shops in a variety of shapes and sizes, but you can easily make your own. Pulls can also be worn within the sleeves of a jacket.

1 To make the "pull", remove the lid from a 35mm film canister and cut a hole about 2cm (¾in) in diameter. Pierce a small hole in the bottom of the canister and, with a simple knot inside, attach a piece of elastic approximately 60cm (24in) long. (The length depends on your waist size. For greater strength, cut double the length and fold the elastic in half.) Attach a safety pin to the free end of the elastic. Put the lid back on the canister.

2 Thread the elastic through your belt loops from your left side around to your right side. Attach the safety pin to a loop on the right of your body. It may take several attempts to find the correct position for the "pull" and the elastic may need to be cut down or adjusted.

3 The canister should rest at a position approximately in line with your trouser pocket, and the tension of the elastic should hold it loosely but firmly against the belt loop. Test the operation of the "pull" by pulling the canister away from the belt loop to a position in front of your chest. Let the canister go, and it should return to the position it started in. If not, readjust the gimmick.

secret view

4 In performance, hold the "pull" in your left hand. Stretch out the elastic so that your left hand can maintain a position just in front of your body. Be careful not to pull open your jacket and reveal your secret – this is an exposed view of the position you should be in.

5 Show the silk handkerchief in your right hand. Pretend to insert it into your left hand. In reality, you are pushing it into the canister through the hole in the lid.

6 Continue pushing the silk into your hand until it is completely contained within the canister.

7 This exposed view shows the position after the silk is inside the gimmick. At this stage, allow the elastic to pull the canister through your fingers and back into your jacket. Keep your hand in a position that still looks as though it holds the silk. Your spectator's view remains as in step 6.

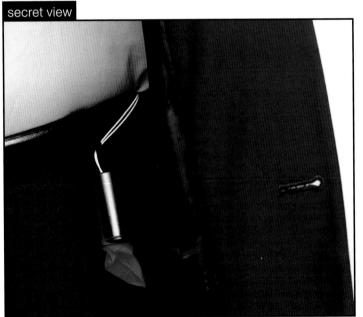

8 The canister rests back where it started, in a position under the jacket by your left pocket.

9 Move both hands to a position in front of your chest and slowly show that they are completely empty. The silk has vanished!

milk to silk

Milk is poured from a jug into a large cup. The cup is turned upside down but the milk mysteriously fails to fall out! The magician reaches into the upturned cup to reveal that the milk has changed into a white silk handkerchief. This trick creates a beautiful effect and is ideal for larger audiences. For added effect, cut white paper into confetti-size pieces and place them in the folds of the silk before placing the handkerchief in the cup. While performing this effect, it is important that you are aware at all times of the position of the cup in relation to your audience. If you hold the cup too low, the secret will be revealed. A cocktail shaker is the ideal size cup to use.

1 To prepare, carefully measure and cut a piece of board that will divide a cup internally in two. The height of the partition should be about three-quarters the height of the cup.

2 Mould some reusable adhesive around the bottom and side edges of the partition.

3 Push the partition into the cup and secure it to the sides with the adhesive. The idea is to create a watertight compartment. If you perform this trick on a regular basis, make the partition longer-lasting by using a sheet of plastic and a silicone sealant.

4 Insert a piece of sponge into one side of the cup. You may need to cut the sponge to shape and experiment to determine how much to use. The best sponge to use is the "super-absorbent" type which holds many times its own weight in liquid.

5 To complete the preparation, push a white silk handkerchief into the other compartment. One corner should be near the top, but make sure it is pushed down out of sight.

6 Place the prepared cup on to a table, along with a jug full of milk.

7 Begin your performance by carefully pouring some milk into the sponge side of the cup. Once again, experimentation will determine exactly how much milk to use. The milk is absorbed by the sponge.

8 It is wise to wait for a few seconds to ensure that the sponge soaks up all of the milk. Place one hand over the mouth of the cup and get ready to turn it upside down.

9 The slickest way to turn the cup is to allow it to swivel between your left fingers and thumb. When it is upside down, freeze for a few seconds as if something might have gone wrong. This creates a moment of tension and humour if acted well.

11 Slowly pull the silk out completely, allowing it to cascade from the cup.

10 Take away your hand from under the mouth of the cup and show that the milk has mysteriously defied gravity. Sometimes a small piece of silk will begin to fall from the cup but this helps to create the illusion that the milk is turning into silk.

the trick which fooled houdini

A borrowed watch is placed under a handkerchief and several spectators confirm its presence. In an instant the watch disappears without a trace. Just as mysteriously, the watch can be made to reappear. Rumour has it that one of the world's most famous magicians, Harry Houdini, was fooled by this trick back in the 1920s!

This is one of the few tricks you will learn which requires an assistant, or "stooge". Choose someone who can act well and whom you can trust to keep the secret.

1 Borrow a watch from a spectator. Place it under the centre of a handkerchief. Ask several people to reach underneath to verify that the watch is indeed still there.

secret view

2 The last person to reach under the handkerchief is your stooge, who secretly takes away the watch. To add a simple piece of "misdirection", move the handkerchief away from your assistant's hand as the secret steal takes place. All eyes will follow the handkerchief.

3 Make a magical gesture and whip the handkerchief away to show that the watch has well and truly gone!

thimble magic

A thimble is compact enough to be carried wherever you go and will generate interest as soon as it is made to appear. By linking several of the effects together, a nice routine can be developed. For instance,

after performing the Linking Paper Clips, you could produce the thimble from the banknote (see opposite) and continue your routine with the Jumping Thimble, finishing with the Vanishing Thimble.

jumping thimble

A thimble magically jumps back and forth between two fingers. Although this is a simple stunt, it is amazing how well the illusion

works. The trick can also be performed with a finger ring, and is a good impromptu stunt to remember.

1 Place a thimble on the tip of the right second finger. Hold the first and second fingers against the palm of your left hand.

2 Tap your fingers against your palm three times. After the second tap, the fingers come approximately 10cm (4in) away from the palm.

3 The first finger quickly curls in and the third finger uncurls.

4 As the fingers reach the palm of the hand, it seems the thimble has jumped. The thimble can be made to jump back by reversing the procedure.

thimble from banknote

A banknote is shown on both sides and rolled into a cone. From within the cone, a thimble is produced. This makes a very startling and highly unusual production. As mentioned previously, stringing various effects together is a nice way to present a small impromptu show, and this is an ideal opening effect. It introduces the thimble unexpectedly and will command interest from your audience.

1 Place a thimble on your right second finger. Hold a banknote with both hands, between your first fingers and thumbs. Curl in your other fingers.

2 From the front, your spectators can see the whole surface of the banknote and the thimble is completely hidden.

3 Turn the note so that you show both sides completely. Be careful not to prematurely expose the thimble.

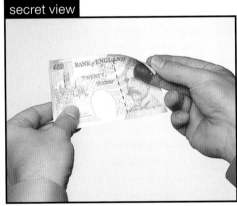

4 Open your second finger so that the thimble rests on the top right of the banknote. The note is clipped against the thimble, between the first and second fingers, and starts to curl in a cone shape.

5 The left hand lifts its end up and over the thimble. It continues to roll the note over and around the second finger, the first finger lifting out of the way.

6 The result is a cone, formed around the second finger of the right hand.

7 Pull out your finger, leaving the thimble within the cone.

8 Dip your finger back into the cone and push it securely into the thimble.

9 Remove your finger from the cone and display the thimble.

thimble thumb clip

A thimble is caused to disappear and then reappear from the tip of the fingers. Anything that fits on the end of your first finger will work perfectly well. For a really impromptu performance, try using a candy wrapper fashioned into a thimble or a hoop-shaped potato chip. The Thimble Thumb Clip is one of the main sleights necessary to master in order to perform many thimble tricks.

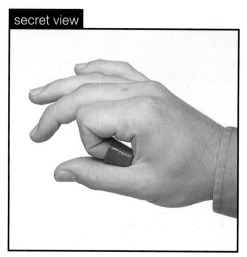

secret view

1 Place a thimble on the tip of your right first finger. Curl your first finger inwards so that the thimble rests in the crotch of your thumb.

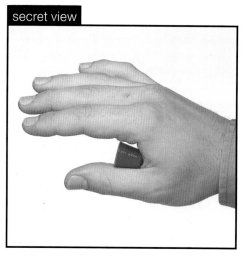

secret view

2 Squeeze your thumb against the thimble and uncurl your finger, leaving the thimble clipped between the base of your thumb and first finger.

3 From the front, the thimble is hidden from view and the hand looks perfectly empty. In performance you will need to be aware of angle restrictions.

vanishing thimble

Once you have learnt the Thimble Thumb Clip, you can try the following routine. When executed correctly, the illusion is superb. When you have mastered the trick of making the thimble reappear from behind your hand, you can easily use the same sleight to make it reappear from anywhere you choose, for example from behind the ear of a child or from inside someone else's pocket.

1 Place a thimble on your right first finger, and hold it against the base of the left fingers. Your left palm should face the audience.

2 Curl in your left second, third and fourth fingers. Open the fingers again to show that the thimble is still there, then start to close the fingers as before.

3 Just as the fingers cover the thimble, begin to remove the right first finger, simultaneously raising the hand and placing the thimble into a Thumb Clip.

4 This view shows the right hand as it moves upwards.

5 The view from the back shows the thimble in the Thumb Clip.

6 Bring the right hand back down to the position shown.

7 Open the left fingers to show that the thimble has vanished. These actions should happen smoothly and briskly. The spectators should not be aware that the thimble has gone from the left fingers until they are opened.

8 Turn the left hand over to show the back of the hand, then show the palm once again.

9 The right hand reaches behind the left and secretly replaces the thumb-clipped thimble on the first finger.

10 This view from the back shows the thimble being recovered.

11 Finish by displaying the thimble back on the fingertip against the palm of the left hand.

thimble from silk

A thimble is produced from a silk, ready to be used for other amazing tricks such as Thimble through Silk. Even though you might not think *this is a startling piece of magic, it is a nice visual way to introduce a thimble; better than simply pulling a thimble out of a pocket.*

secret view

1 Hold a thimble in the right-hand Thumb Clip position. Display a silk handkerchief, stretching it between the two top corners with both hands.

2 From the front, all the fingers and the entire silk can be seen, and the thimble remains completely hidden.

3 Cross your arms to show the back of the silk, then uncross your arms again.

secret view

4 Hold the silk by a corner in the left hand. Your right hand reaches under the silk and retrieves the thimble from the Thumb Clip.

5 Drape the silk momentarily over your right first finger.

6 Whip away the silk to display a thimble on your fingertip.

thimble through silk

A thimble is placed under a silk and visibly melts through the fabric. This trick is the perfect follow-up to Thimble from Silk. Although it is not easy to learn or perform, it is beautiful to watch when performed well. Use a thimble that contrasts with the colour of the silk.

secret view

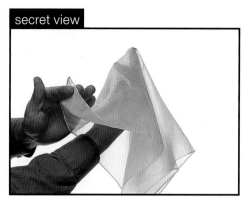
secret view

1 Hold a silk handkerchief with your left hand. It should be clipped between the first and second fingers, draping down the inside of the hand. The right hand displays a thimble on the first fingertip.

2 Hold the silk about chest level and start to move the thimble under the silk. As it passes the left hand, the thimble is secretly placed into the left-hand Thumb Clip position.

3 Without hesitation, continue to move the finger under the silk to a position in the centre. Under cover of the silk, extend your second finger and bend your first finger backwards. This can be seen here through the silk for ease of explanation.

secret view

4 Make a gesture with your left hand, which positions itself directly behind the right hand.

5 During this gesture, push the thimble from the Thumb Clip on to the first finger through the silk. In this view, the silk is lifted for ease of explanation.

secret view

6 The first finger straightens behind the second finger. Care must be taken to keep the thimble hidden.

7 From the front, the thimble remains totally unseen.

8 With a shake of the hand, lower the second finger so that the thimble pops into view.

paper magic

A most versatile material, paper is easily available and comes in a wide variety of shapes, colours, sizes and thicknesses. Of the many tricks that use paper, a few are given here which are simple to prepare, and very enjoyable to watch. As well as working as close-up tricks, Cut and Restored Newspaper, together with Snowstorm in China, can work on stage because they can be seen from a distance.

telekinetic paper

A small piece of paper is folded and stood upright on a table. Apparently using nothing but the power of the human mind, the paper is made to fall over. Is this a true demonstration of telekinesis? No, but it certainly looks like it!

1 For this trick, you will need a small piece of paper, approximately 6 x 3cm (2¼ x 1¼in). The exact size is unimportant but the success of this trick depends on the height of the paper being sufficiently more than the width. Fold the paper in half along its length.

2 Open up the fold to form a "V" shape and position the paper about arm's length in front of you. Due to the height of the paper, it is relatively easy to secretly offset its balance and make it fall over. Rub your first and second finger on your arm, explaining that you are harnessing some static electricity.

3 Gently swing your arm to a position directly in front of the paper but about 15cm (6in) away. As your arm swings around, the air will move and cause the paper to become unstable. As you are a little distance away, the change in air current will take one or two seconds to reach the paper – this will also help to disguise the method to this trick.

4 The paper will fall to the table. Try experimenting with the distance you place between your fingers and the paper. The further away you are, the better the illusion looks. Despite the fact that the method is very simple, the trick itself is extremely baffling – as you will see when you try this out for yourself.

cut and restored newspaper

A strip of newspaper is unmistakably snipped into two pieces, yet is instantly shown to be restored. This is an ideal trick for a larger audience. It can be performed for a group of children or adults with equal success.

To add to the presentation, invite a member of the audience to participate. Give them a pair of scissors and a normal strip of newspaper and ask them to follow your actions carefully. You will always succeed and they will always fail. This effect can be very comical.

If you plan your moves carefully, after a few demonstrations you could switch your strip with theirs and have the spectator "unexpectedly" succeed. This would be a great finish to the routine.

1 To prepare, cut a strip of newspaper from the financial section. The content of such a page will help to camouflage the join. Place the newspaper on top of a scrap of paper to protect the table. Apply a thin layer of rubber cement glue to the middle section of the strip, as shown here.

2 Wait for the glue to dry completely, then apply some talcum powder to the covered area. This will stop the glued surface of the strip prematurely sticking at the wrong moment. Blow any excess powder off the newspaper so that everything looks normal.

3 The final piece of preparation is to fold the strip in half with a sharp crease.

4 To begin the performance, display the strip of newspaper in one hand and the scissors in the other.

5 Fold the strip in half along the crease and clearly snip off about 1cm (½in) from the centre. Try to make the cut as straight as possible. Because of the rubber cement glue, the two separate pieces will be glued back together at the join.

6 Open the strip and the paper will have magically restored itself. You can stop here or repeat the cutting and restoring process. It all depends how much of the strip you covered in glue.

7 Instead of cutting the paper straight, experiment by cutting it at a right angle. You can also place the glue at strategically placed points on the strip of newspaper so that you can begin by actually cutting the strip into two pieces. Then place the two pieces together, cutting again to re-join them.

snowstorm in china

Several sheets of tissue paper are displayed and torn into strips. They are soaked in a glass of water and squeezed dry. An ornamental Chinese fan is used to aid the drying process and the paper begins to turn into confetti, creating a mini snowstorm that fills the air and covers the stage. This is a spectacular closing effect for a show.

There are several versions of this traditional trick. The following method is the invention of a wonderful Hungarian magician, the Great Kovari. We graciously thank him for allowing us to share his method with you. Many top professional magicians feature versions of this trick in their act.

1 To prepare, cut a strip of flexible plastic, approximately 1 x 10cm (½ x 4in). Pierce a small hole in the centre with a sharp point.

2 Attach a short length of thread to the plastic strip by tying it in a knot through the hole.

3 Use adhesive tape to attach the thread to the back of a fan so that the plastic strip hangs down behind the centre.

4 Make a hole in the top of an egg and empty the inside. Wash it out and let it dry completely before continuing.

5 Cut some coloured tissue paper into confetti-size pieces. Carefully pack them into the egg.

6 Bend the plastic strip in half, then place it carefully into the hole in the egg so that when the strip expands it grips the sides of the egg securely.

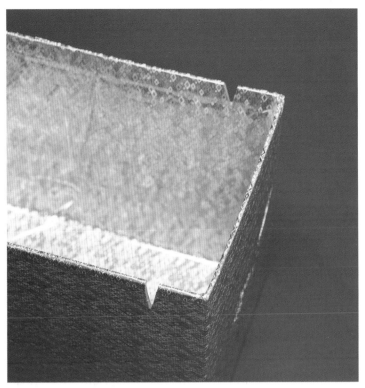

7 Cut two notches into the sides of a box. These will function as a display stand for the fan, as well as a secret holder for the wet tissue.

8 Set a table with the fan displayed in the box, a glass of water to the left and some tissue paper sheets at the back of the box. From the back, you can also see the egg hanging from the fan.

9 From the front, there is a pretty display of props and the egg remains hidden behind the fan.

10 To perform, display the various coloured sheets of tissue paper and clearly tear them into shreds. ▶

11 Roll up the shreds into a ball and drop it into the glass, soaking the paper thoroughly.

12 Replace the glass on the table and display the wet ball of paper in your right fingertips. Squeeze it dry.

13 Now make a fake transfer into your left hand. Place the ball of paper against the fingers of your open left hand and close it as your right hand comes away with the ball hidden behind the fingers.

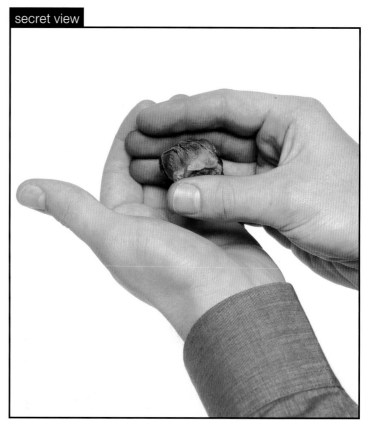

14 This close-up view shows the position of the hands as they come together. Your body movement should suggest that the ball of paper is really in the left hand.

secret view

15 The right hand drops the wad of soggy paper into the box as it reaches for the fan.

16 This view from the back shows the paper being dropped as the hand reaches for the bottom of the fan.

17 Hold the fan up with the left hand hidden behind it. Say that you are going to dry the paper by fanning it.

secret view

18 With the left hand, secretly pull the egg off the plastic strip. The fan provides a great deal of cover for this.

19 Squeeze the egg tightly, breaking the shell, as you rapidly wave the fan to distribute the confetti pieces as far and wide as possible. The broken eggshell will drop to the floor with the paper, and the evidence will not be noticed. All that is left to do is tidy up!

money
magic

Money is the one thing that most people carry with them at all times. The following pages reveal some wonderful magic tricks for you to perform. Have you ever dreamed of making money appear from nowhere at your fingertips, or of being able to change a blank piece of paper into a banknote? If so, your dreams are about to come true – or so your audience will believe!

- easy money tricks
- basic coin techniques
- coin vanishes
- more money tricks

introduction

Rightly or wrongly, the one thing most people desire in their lives, along with health and happiness, is money. If we could really perform magic, we would make money appear so that we could live the life of our dreams and help others live theirs. The idea of producing money out of thin air was born a long time ago, and magicians over the years have devised countless ways of creating this illusion.

Towards the end of the nineteenth century, one of the most skilled coin manipulators of all time created an act entitled "The Miser's Dream". His name was Thomas Nelson Downs and he billed himself as the "King of Koins". The act is said to have lasted about 30 minutes and contained only coin magic. His act was so popular that he left his American homeland in 1899 and travelled throughout Europe, where he found further fame and success. Part of his act involved showing his hands completely empty, removing his hat, showing that empty too, then producing coin after coin after coin. Each coin was thrown into the hat until it was full of money. "The Ariel Treasury", as it was then called, is now better known by magicians as "The Miser's Dream", in remembrance of the late, great T. Nelson Downs. It is still being performed regularly today, and is received as well now as it was then.

For general coin tricks and coin manipulation you can use any coins that may be to hand, but magicians favour the American half-dollar for its size, weight and

Above: You too can learn how to produce money at your fingertips from out of thin air!

Left: An early poster publicizing the master coin manipulator Thomas Nelson Downs (1867–1938), also known as the "King of Koins". Many theatres and agents were dubious about booking an act comprising only coin tricks, thinking that it would be too monotonous and that the coins would not be seen easily in a large theatre. However, Downs proved the sceptics wrong when his performances caused a sensation wherever he worked.

Above: Magicians all over the world have been performing magic with coins for centuries. Coins are available in all shapes, sizes and colours, and they are easy to find at any time.

Above: No matter where you are in the world, you will always be prepared to amaze and amuse with a few banknotes and a little knowledge of the secrets in this book.

gripping qualities. The milled edge makes it relatively easy to palm and manipulate. Try to choose shiny coins to maximize their visibility. Old coin shops are often a great source for a variety of different coins in all manner of shapes, sizes and colours. Introducing such items to your audiences will cause interest. You may even be able to build a presentation around the existence of the coin. Where does it originate from? How did you come to possess it?

The following pages reveal how to make banknotes and coins appear and disappear (Appearing Money, Handkerchief Coin Vanish), how to cause coins to change places (Switcheroo) and bend (Bending Coin, Versions 1 and 2), and even how to turn a piece of blank paper into a banknote (Paper to Money). Basic sleight of hand is explained, and with the knowledge of a few of these routines you will always be able to perform a trick or two.

Above: Make a coin melt through the centre of a silk handkerchief without any damage whatsoever.

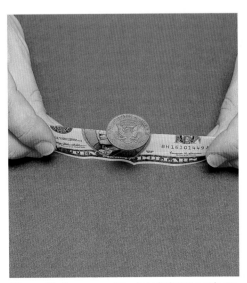

Above: Challenge your friends to balance a coin on the edge of a banknote.

Above: Make a banknote defy gravity by floating it above your hand. No strings attached!

easy money tricks

All of the tricks described in this chapter require money. Thankfully, the only thing you will actually have to invest is your time in order to learn the tricks described. The first few tricks are easy to learn and

perform. They fall into the area of impromptu magic, since they require no special set-up or gimmicks. You can perform these easy money tricks at the drop of a hat.

linking paper clips

Two paperclips and a rubber band are hooked on to a banknote. The three separate objects instantly link together! This is an old classic of

magic and only requires everyday objects, so is ideal for those occasions when you are suddenly asked to perform unprepared.

1 Fold one-third of a banknote under itself and attach a paperclip at the edge.

2 Place a rubber band over the note, at approximately the centre, as shown here.

3 Fold the other side of the note in the opposite direction to the first fold. Using a second paperclip, clip this edge to the top layer of the fold made earlier.

4 Grip both sides of the banknote and gently pull your hands apart until the banknote is stretched out flat.

5 The result is a rubber band with two paperclips linked together, hanging from a banknote. It seems impossible. The three items link so quickly that it will take your spectators completely by surprise.

bending coin (version 1)

A coin is examined and then held in the fingertips. The magician creates an optical illusion which makes the coin look as if it is bending like rubber. This effect can be followed by Version 2, which appears later in this chapter. To accompany the trick, you could explain that although a coin is made of metal and therefore solid, the magical warmth of your hands can cause it to melt!

1 Hold a coin with both hands, thumbs on the back of the coin, first and second fingers on the front. Allow as much of the coin's surface as possible to be seen by pushing the thumbs forward and pulling the edges of the coin back.

2 This is the view from above, and it can be seen that a good deal of the front surface of the coin is visible.

3 Move both hands inwards so that the backs of your hands move towards each other. The thumbs maintain contact with the coin at all times. Move your hands back to the position shown in step 2 and repeat the motion five or six times.

heads I win!

A pocket full of change is emptied on to the table and a small selection of coins chosen. While the magician looks away (or leaves the room) the spectator is instructed to turn over two coins at a time, as many times as desired. Finally they are asked to hide one of the coins under their hand before the magician returns. The magician is able to reveal, with absolute accuracy, whether the hidden coin is heads up or tails up!

1 Throw some change on to a table. You can use any number of coins, but six or seven is perfect. Note whether there are an even or odd number of coins facing heads up. In our example, there are three heads up so we simply remember "Heads are odd".

2 Turn your back and instruct the spectator to turn over two coins at a time, as many times as desired. All the while, keep remembering "Heads are odd". Ask for any one of the coins to be covered before you turn around.

3 Glance at the uncovered coins on the table to see how many coins are now heads up. In our example, there are three. Remember "Heads are odd"? If there are an odd number left, then the hidden coin must be tails up. If there were an even number remaining heads up, then the hidden coin would also be heads up.

4 Assume a hypnotic state, or pretend to receive psychic vibes, then reveal the orientation of the hidden coin. If your instructions have been followed correctly, Heads I Win! will work every single time. Most people carry small change with them, so you can perform this trick at a moment's notice.

explanation
The reason this trick works is because the coins are turned over two at a time, so if there are an odd number of heads facing up at the beginning there will be an odd number of heads facing up at the end, and vice versa.

impossible coin balance

This is a perfect way to win a drink! Challenge your friends to balance a coin on the edge of a banknote. The chances are, no matter how hard they try or how many different ways they attempt to tackle the problem, they will not succeed unless they know the secret.

1 The success of this stunt relies on the use of a crisp banknote. Fold and sharply crease the note in half, along its length.

2 Fold the note in half again, this time along the width. Ensure that the creases are sharp and neat.

3 Place the note on a table so that the folded edge is pointing upwards. Position a coin on top of the "V" shape. You may even amaze yourself with the next part!

4 Slowly and gently pull both edges of the note away from each other, straightening the paper. The coin will always find its centre of balance and will remain on the folded edge of the note, in an apparently impossible position.

explanation
In reality, the short crease is never pulled completely flat and the tiny kink in the paper is enough to stop the coin from falling off. Once the banknote is stretched flat, a steady hand is vital for the success of this trick.

floating banknote

A banknote is held in the fingertips and caused to float away from the hand without any visible means of support. There are many versions of this trick, and nearly all of them are difficult to master.

However, this particular version is surprisingly easy to learn and can be performed at the drop of a hat with only a few seconds of preparation before you begin.

1 To prepare, take a piece of reusable adhesive and attach it to the centre of a banknote.

2 To begin the performance, pick up the note so that the adhesive sticks to your right second fingertip.

3 Rub the note between the palms of both hands, explaining that you are generating static electricity.

secret view

4 Slowly remove your left hand, showing the banknote adhering to your right fingers. Begin to spread the right fingers, simultaneously bending your second finger inwards, which will move the note away from the palm of the hand. From the front, it appears as if the note is floating away from the hand and hovering in mid-air. Watch this in a mirror to see how good it looks.

5 When your second finger is fully extended, the note seems to be floating quite a long way in front of the hand.

6 This view from above shows what is really happening. To finish, slowly bring both hands together again as in step 3, then put the note in your pocket or secretly remove the adhesive and hand out the banknote for examination.

basic coin techniques

Now that you have learnt some easy money tricks, it is time to learn a few sleight-of-hand techniques that will enable you to perform some even more amazing magic. Many of these techniques will take time and practice to master, but the outcome is most rewarding. As suggested earlier in the book, practising in a mirror will make it much easier for you to correct your own mistakes.

finger palm and production

The Finger Palm is an essential grip in coin magic, allowing you to secretly hold and therefore hide a coin (or any small object) in your hand. The coin can then be made to appear from anywhere, using the Finger Palm Production (for example, from behind a child's ear).

1 Position the coin at the base of your right second and third fingers. It is held in place by the creases in your skin and by your fingers curling in to hold it. Try to forget that you are holding a coin – look in a mirror to see if you can hold your hand naturally by your side. Your hand should not look as though it were holding anything.

2 You can produce the coin in many different ways. One way is to pretend that you have spotted something floating in the air in front of you. Point it out with the hand that is secretly holding the coin.

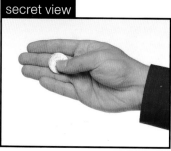
secret view

3 As you reach for the invisible "something", use your thumb to push the coin from its position at the base of your fingers to the fingertips.

4 Try to allow as much of the coin to be seen as possible. The coin seems to appear during the movement between pointing at the floating object and you reaching for it.

5 From the front, it looks just as if you have plucked a coin from thin air.

thumb clip

This is another technique for gripping a coin secretly in your hand. It can also be used to "vanish" a coin. The beauty of this grip is that it allows wide movement of the fingers, while convincingly keeping the coin out of sight.

1 Begin by resting the coin on the right fingers. It should lie flat, in the middle of the first and second fingers.

secret view

2 Close the fingers into a fist. The coin almost automatically ends in a position which can be clipped by the thumb.

secret view

3 With the hand open, the coin remains hidden from the front. This exposed view shows the Thumb-Clipped coin.

classic palm

This is one of the most useful sleights to learn. It enables the performer to hide any small object (in this case a coin) in the palm of the hand, without its presence being detected. The most important aspect of any Palm is that the hand must appear natural, so do not hold your hand in an awkward position or move in a way which attracts attention. A common problem is that both the thumb and fourth finger will try to flare out at an unnatural angle, but this will happen less as you learn to relax your hand. After enough practice, your hand will develop tiny muscles that will help you to palm. A palmed object should not be gripped tightly; a gentle touch is all that is required.

1 Place a coin on your outstretched hand. It should lie flat on the tips of the second and third fingers.

2 Keep the fingers parallel to the ground as you turn your hand palm down. The coin should be directly below the palm of your hand.

3 Push the coin into your palm with your second and third fingertips. The exact position of the coin is crucial to success. You may have to move it about a few times and try the coin in slightly different areas of the palm until you feel comfortable.

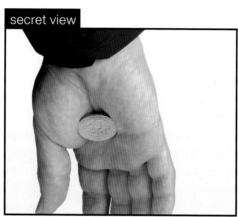

secret view

4 Remove the second and third fingers from the coin, trapping the coin in the palm by gently squeezing the edges between the fleshy pad of the thumb and the area of skin at the opposite edge of the coin.

secret view

5 This view shows the correct position of the coin. The coin need not be pinched hard. Only a gentle pressure is needed to stop the coin from falling.

6 The coin can be held in the Classic Palm without detection, as long as it looks natural.

7 In this example, the distortion of the hand is totally unnatural and therefore a clear sign that it hides something.

secret view

8 Continue your everyday activities (such as writing, typing and eating) with a coin palmed, and you will soon learn to forget it is there.

downs palm

The Downs Palm is named after the nineteenth-century American magician Thomas Nelson Downs, who is still recognized as one of the finest manipulators of coins ever. This grip is very deceptive as you can show both the front and back of the hand empty before producing a coin. There are angle problems, however, and anyone viewing from

too high or too low may glimpse the hidden coin. Practise and check your movements in the mirror – before long you will develop an instinct as to whether or not the coin can be seen.

Performed well, this creates a beautiful effect. The coin can be plucked from the air or from any suitable location.

1 Grip the coin between the tips of the right first and second fingers.

2 As the hand closes, the coin should naturally position itself in the crotch of the thumb.

3 Open the fingers, leaving the coin gripped in the web between the thumb and the first finger.

4 You can show your hand from both front and back without the coin being seen, as long as you keep the correct angle in relation to the audience.

downs palm production

1 To produce the coin, reverse the above moves. Close your hand, ensuring that the edge of the coin becomes gripped between the tips of the first and second fingers, as seen here.

2 Open your hand, bringing the tip of your thumb on to the edge of the coin and keeping this contact as your hand continues to open.

3 Finally, pinch the coin between your thumb and second finger. Steps 1, 2 and 3 should happen together in one seamless movement.

bobo switch

This is a method of switching one coin for another. It was invented by French magician J.B. Bobo in about 1900, and is still used widely today. The switch is not used as a trick by itself, but being able to switch your coin for a spectator's is an invaluable tool. Bending Coin (Version 2) is an example of the use of the Bobo Switch. Study the following explanation carefully and it will not take too long to learn.

secret view

1 Hold the coin to be switched in the right-hand Finger Palm position. Borrow a coin from a spectator and hold it clearly displayed in the right fingertips. Hold the left hand out flat.

2 From the front, the secret coin is completely hidden in the right palm.

secret view

3 The switch occurs as the right hand tosses the borrowed coin into the left hand. It goes unnoticed because the coin is in motion the entire time. The right second and third fingers extend to cover the coin and the secret coin is allowed to fall from the Finger Palm position to the outstretched left hand.

secret view

4 Without hesitation, the right thumb pulls the borrowed coin into the Finger Palm position, and the left hand closes around the switched coin.

5 From the front, the action of tossing the coin from one hand to the other looks very natural and should not arouse any suspicion from your audience.

6 Slowly open your left hand to show that the coin has been switched.

coin roll

This flourish is a well-known favourite with audiences worldwide. A coin is rolled across the knuckles in a flourish which looks as magical as it is beautiful. The Coin Roll is a wonderful example of digital dexterity; it is also one of the most difficult things you will *learn in this book. You can practise it while you are watching television. Once you have mastered it, try learning it with the other hand and perform two Coin Rolls simultaneously! It is possible to perform the Coin Roll with four coins, each coin rotating ahead of the next.*

1 Close your hand into a loose fist. Your knuckles should be parallel with the floor. Begin by balancing a coin on the tip of your thumb.

2 Pinch your thumb against the side of your first finger so that the coin flips on to its edge.

3 Loosen your thumb's grip on the coin so that it balances on the back of the first finger. At the same time, raise your second, third and fourth fingers just enough to clip the coin's edge between the first and second fingers.

4 Raise your first and third fingers while lowering the second finger. This allows you to roll the coin across the back of the second finger.

5 Lower the third finger and raise the second and fourth fingers. The coin will roll across the back of the third finger. Allow the coin to flip over and rest on the side of your fourth finger.

6 Move your thumb under your hand, towards the coin.

7 The coin is transferred to the tip of the thumb, which carries it back under the hand to the start position.

8 You are now in a position to repeat the sequence again.

coin vanishes

There are countless ways to make a coin vanish. The French Drop, Fake Take and Thumb Clip Vanish are all sleight-of-hand methods and generally should not be used as tricks in their own right. As you become more experienced, you will find that you can incorporate the coin's disappearance into a longer sequence, which can be extra mystifying and a lot of fun.

french drop

This is one of the oldest and best-known techniques used to "vanish" a coin or any other small object. The coin is held in the fingertips of the left hand and supposedly taken by the right hand. In reality, the coin is secretly retained in the left hand. This move should not be shown as a trick on its own, but as a way of "vanishing" a coin within another trick.

1 Display a coin by holding it high in the left fingertips. As much as possible of the surface of the coin should be seen.

2 The right hand approaches the left to supposedly take the coin. The thumb goes under it while the fingers go over it.

3 As soon as the fingers close around the coin and it is out of view, let the coin fall into the left hand.

secret view

4 The coin falls between the right thumb and the back of the left fingers, almost in Finger Palm position.

5 From the front, it looks as though you pinch the coin with your right fingers and thumb. Watch the coin yourself and actually believe that you are taking the coin.

6 Move the right hand up and to your right, at the same time allowing the left hand (with the coin) to drop naturally to your side. Follow your right hand with your eyes. Your hand should look as though it is actually holding a coin.

7 Squeeze your right hand slowly, supposedly shrinking the coin. Open the fingers wide and show the coin is no longer there.

tip To make the move more convincing, place a pencil on a table, off to your left-hand side. Hold the coin in the start position. Execute the French Drop, then immediately use your left hand to pick up the pencil. Tap your right hand with the pencil, then show that the coin has vanished. Using the pencil like a wand provides a reason for taking the coin with your right hand – it is more natural to pick up the pencil using your left hand than to reach across your body with your right hand. When executing a sleight, it is very important to justify moves which may look strange if made without a reason.

thumb clip vanish

This creates the illusion of placing a coin in your left hand while you secretly retain it in your right hand. It makes use of the technique in magic known as "time misdirection". If you leave enough time between secretly retaining the coin and showing that it has "vanished", the audience will not be able to remember the last time they actually saw the coin or in which hand they saw it. This makes it very difficult for them to reconstruct the method. "Time misdirection" can be applied to many other secret moves and routines.

1 Display a coin on your right fingertips in preparation for the Thumb Clip.

2 Display your open left hand at waist level. Move the left hand up. At the same time begin to close the right hand, placing the coin into the Thumb Clip.

3 Supposedly place the coin on to the fingertips of the left hand, but secretly retain the coin in your right hand.

secret view

4 This view from behind shows what is happening.

secret view

5 As the right hand moves away from the left and drops to your side, the left fingers close around the "coin". Your eyes must follow your left hand and your body language should suggest that the coin really is in this hand. This exposed view shows the coin in the right hand; in performance it would be hidden in the Thumb Clip or would be allowed to drop into the Finger Palm position.

6 The left hand moves away from your body, to the left. Open the hand and show that the coin has disappeared.

7 To make the move look more natural, give your right hand something to do after it leaves the left hand. Pick up a pencil with the coin in the Thumb Clip. Tap your left hand with the pencil, then show that the coin has gone. Even better, have the pencil in your right pocket and, as you take out the pencil, leave the coin in your pocket.

fake take

Like the French Drop and the Thumb Clip Vanish, the Fake Take enables you to secretly retain an object in one hand while supposedly taking it in the other hand. Try to provide a reason for taking the coin in the right hand – for example, to pick something up with the other hand. This type of sleight should not be used as a trick in its own

right, but as part of a longer routine. In some routines the French Drop or Thumb Clip Vanish will be more suitable than the Fake Take. However, it is important to learn several ways to achieve a similar result so that you can choose which looks best. It will not necessarily be the same technique every time.

1 Display a coin on the outstretched fingers of your left hand at about waist height. The coin should be in a position ready for a Finger Palm.

2 The right hand approaches the left hand, supposedly to take the coin. The right fingers lie flat on top of the coin.

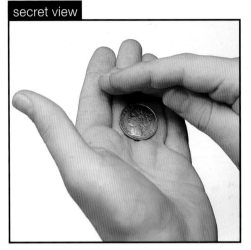

secret view

3 The left hand begins to close as the right hand feigns pinching the coin with the thumb against the fingers. This view from behind shows that in reality the coin remains in exactly the same position, ready to be finger-palmed by the left hand.

4 The right hand swings to the right (with the back towards the audience) as the left hand drops to your left side, supposedly empty, holding the coin in a Finger Palm.

5 As the right hand moves across your body, watch it as you would if the coin was really there. Your body language should suggest that the coin really is in your right hand.

6 Slowly open your right hand to show that the coin has vanished.

sleeving a coin

Magicians are always accused of using their sleeves to secretly hide objects. In fact very few tricks rely on this method, known as "sleeving". There are many different sleeving techniques. If you perfect this method, you will be able to make a coin disappear instantly without the need for any gimmicks. The only requirement is that you wear a jacket with loose-fitting sleeves. The trick will take lots of practice to perfect, and many people give up too soon. If you persevere, you will be rewarded handsomely with a baffling quick trick which will amaze all who see it. Sometimes, even when you know how a trick is done, it still looks magical. Such is the case here.

secret view

1 Close your left fingers into a fist. Place a coin on the back of your hand. The coin must be parallel with the ground, otherwise it may fall off.

2 Hold your right fingers above the coin. Snap your fingers. As your right second finger snaps off the thumb, it strikes the coin. With practice, if you strike the coin correctly it will automatically sail through the air and up your right sleeve.

3 As soon as the sound of the snap is heard, the coin seems to melt away. Try to keep your left hand perfectly still and as soon as the coin disappears, freeze, so that your spectator doesn't think you tried to sneak the coin away with your right hand.

secret view

4 Show both hands back and front. They are unmistakably empty. Keep the right arm slightly bent and be careful not to let the coin fall out of your sleeve.

5 You can retrieve the coin by allowing your right arm to hang by your side. The coin will fall from your sleeve and you can catch it in the Finger Palm position.

coin in elbow

You hold a coin in your fingertips and rub it against your elbow. After several apparently unsuccessful attempts the coin seems to *dissolve into your elbow, disappearing completely. This is another good example of how "misdirection" works.*

1 This is best performed sitting at a table, although you could perform it standing if you alter the handling slightly. Hold a coin in your right fingertips and bend your left arm. (Your left hand should be in a position next to your left ear.) Rub the coin against your elbow. After a few seconds, let the coin fall to the table.

2 Pick up the coin with your left hand and display it on the fingers as you explain that you will try again. Pick up the coin from the left fingers with the right hand. This should be done to look identical to the Fake Take described earlier, which is the move you will be performing later in the trick.

3 Once again repeat the rubbing sequence, only to let the coin fall to the table again. Your audience will become accustomed to these moves, which will help you to accomplish what happens next.

4 Just as before, go to pick up the coin with your left hand and display it in the left fingertips. However, as the right hand approaches to take the coin from the left, execute a Fake Take. Briefly the right fingers mime taking the coin while the left hand returns to a position near the left ear.

secret view

7 Display both hands to complete the "vanish". The coin can be recovered later. It will either stay under your collar or fall down your back. Make sure your shirt is tucked in, or the coin may fall out!

5 This exposed view shows the coin in the left hand. Secretly slip the coin under the back of your shirt collar to dispose of it. Plenty of "misdirection" is caused by the movement of the right hand, which furiously rubs the supposed coin into the elbow.

6 After a few more seconds of rubbing, show that the right hand is empty. The coin has apparently been absorbed into your arm.

handkerchief coin vanish

A coin is placed under a handkerchief and held by a spectator. The handkerchief is shaken out and the coin seems to melt away. A specially prepared handkerchief is required. Cut a corner from a duplicate handkerchief. Stitch it neatly into one of the corners of the handkerchief along three sides. Before stitching the final side, drop a coin into the secret pocket.

secret view

1 Show the coin held in the right fingertips. The handkerchief is opened and held by both hands. The special corner is held in the right hand together with the coin. Your right fingers hide the secret pocket.

2 As you move the coin under the handkerchief (aim for the centre), take the hidden coin with it. Ask a spectator to hold the coin through the fabric. They will assume they are holding the one shown originally, but it is really the duplicate coin sewn into the corner.

3 Allow the loose coin to fall into the Finger Palm position, then remove your hand from the handkerchief in a natural manner.

4 Hold one corner of the handkerchief in each hand and ask the spectator to drop the coin on your command. Count to three and say "Let go!"

5 As they do so, the coin seems to melt away and the handkerchief can be displayed completely empty. You can finish by folding it up and putting it back in your pocket.

clever coin vanish

A coin is placed under a handkerchief and held by a spectator. When the handkerchief is shaken out, the coin melts away. The effect is the same as in Handkerchief Coin Vanish, but the method is very different. This is true of many tricks: there are, for example, dozens of ways of sawing a woman in half! Next time you think you know how a trick is done, take a closer look and see if you really do.

1 To prepare, secretly place a coin into the lining of your tie so that it lies down by the tip.

2 To begin the performance, show another coin in your right hand and an opaque handkerchief in your left.

secret view

3 Place this coin under the handkerchief, taking the tip of your tie with it. Practise this in front of a mirror.

secret view

4 Hold the handkerchief at approximately waist height and close to your body so that your tie continues to hang naturally. If you lift your tie too high, your audience will see what you are doing.

5 Ask a spectator to hold the coin, which is really the one in the tie. As in Handkerchief Coin Vanish, allow the other coin to fall into the Finger Palm position, then casually remove your hand.

6 Hold one corner of the handkerchief in each hand and ask the spectator to let go. Display the handkerchief completely empty and hand it to the spectator for examination. They will find nothing.

tip For a complete "vanish", simply hide the coin in the lining of your tie as you place it under the handkerchief. This way you will not have to palm anything. The use of your tie is so subtle that the method will never be guessed by your spectators.

coin wrap

A coin is wrapped in a piece of paper. It can be seen and even felt until the final moment when the paper is torn into pieces and the coin seems to have vanished without a trace. This is an ideal way to "vanish" a

marked, borrowed coin, which can then be made to appear in another trick later on in your act (for example, Coin in Egg and Coin in Bread Roll). This is a baffling "any time" coin trick worth learning.

1 You will require an opaque piece of paper approximately 9cm (3½in) square. Place a coin into the centre of the paper.

2 Fold the paper upwards against the bottom of the coin with a sharp crease.

3 Fold the paper to the right and back, behind the coin. Make the creases as sharp as possible.

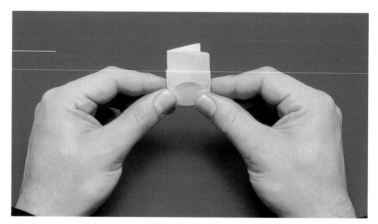

4 Repeat with the left side of the paper. Be careful not to wrap the coin too tightly, as this will hinder the secret move.

5 Fold the top flap back, at the edge of the paper. It seems as if the coin is trapped, but in reality it can escape from the top of the paper where a gap has been left.

6 Press the coin against the paper with your thumbs, turning the package end over end as you do so. This will position the opening of the packet towards the bottom, while creating an impression of the coin on the paper, proving its presence.

7 Have a spectator verify that the coin is still there. Carefully note the position of the paper at this point.

8 Release your thumb's grip, allowing the coin to fall from the paper. The back of your right hand provides a good deal of cover.

9 The coin lands in the right-hand Finger Palm position. It should fall easily from the paper. If not, your folds at steps 3 and 4 may have been too tight.

10 Tear the paper in half, then into quarters. The coin remains hidden in the Finger Palm.

11 Toss the pieces of paper on to the table to complete the "vanish". Make the coin reappear in a place of your choice (*see* More Money Tricks for ideas).

coin vanish from matchbox

A coin is placed inside an empty matchbox. The box is shaken to prove the contents are still there, but moments later the box is shown empty. You can then choose any method you like to make the coin reappear.

You could also adapt the method used in Vanishing Box of Matches (see Match Magic) to add to this routine, enhancing the illusion of the coin being in the box even after it has gone.

1 Open the drawer of an empty matchbox. Insert a coin and display it clearly.

2 Hold the matchbox in your left hand and close the drawer, trapping the coin.

3 Transfer the box to your palm-down right hand.

4 Shake the box by turning your right hand over and back several times. The coin will rattle, proving its presence.

secret view

5 Rattle the box again, but as the hand turns palm up, squeeze the sides of the box so that the top of the box bows open just enough to let the coin slip out into your right hand. This secret move can be disguised by tilting the hand upwards and towards you slightly.

secret view

6 The coin is secretly retained in the Finger Palm position.

8 The left first finger pushes open the drawer to show that the coin has vanished. The box can be dismantled and checked by the audience. There will be nothing to find.

7 As the wrist is turned over again, the box is transferred back into the left hand. The left hand holds the box between the thumb and second finger.

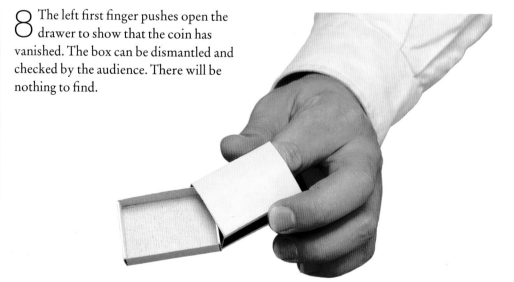

pencil and coin vanish

A coin is held in the fingertips and tapped three times with a pencil. Unexpectedly, the pencil disappears and is found behind the magician's ear! The coin is tapped again and vanishes completely. This routine can be performed at any time, anywhere. Instead of a coin, you can use anything small enough to hide in your hand. This routine is a practical example of how "misdirection" works. It is also a "sucker" trick in that your audience thinks they are let into the secret when in reality you still manage to amaze them.

1 Hold a coin on the outstretched palm of your left hand. Hold a pencil in your right hand. Stand with the left side of your body towards the audience.

2 Tell everyone to watch carefully. Tap the coin three times, each time bringing the pencil up towards your right ear.

secret view

3 On the third tap, without any hesitation, leave the pencil behind your ear. The first two taps are made to build the expectation that the coin is going to vanish.

4 As your hand descends to tap the coin, open it wide and look amazed as you seem to realize at the same time as your audience that the pencil is no longer there.

5 Explain that you should never reveal the secret to a magic trick, but that you are going to break that rule. Turn your body so that your right side is now towards your audience. Point out the pencil behind your ear.

secret view

6 As you do this, secretly place the coin into your left trouser pocket.

7 Explain that you will do the trick again. Return to the position you were in before, with your left side to the audience. Your left hand should be closed as if it holds the coin. Tap your hand three times with the pencil, then open it to show that this time the coin really has gone.

tip *The success of this trick relies on the spectators convincing themselves that the coin is going to vanish. They will be so focused on watching the coin that they will fail to watch the pencil!*

more money tricks

This section explains the methods to various tricks that require some of the knowledge learnt so far. Coin in Egg uses the Coin Wrap vanish and Bending Coin (Version 2) utilizes the Bobo Switch, while several use palming techniques. The final magic trick in the book, Paper to Money, does not require difficult sleight of hand, but is a very strong, visual illusion which you can perform at any time.

switcheroo

In this trick you introduce a game of hand-eye co-ordination. A coin is held on the outstretched palm of a spectator. You explain that you are going to try to grab it before the spectator can close their hand.

You manage to grab the coin twice, but fail on the third attempt. When the spectator opens their hand, they see you have not only removed the coin, but have replaced it with a different coin!

1 For this trick, you will need two different coins. Place one coin on the palm of a spectator's hand.

2 Hold the second coin classic-palmed in your right hand. Details regarding the Classic Palm can be found in Basic Coin Techniques.

3 Explain that you will try to grab the coin before the spectator closes their hand, and that they are not allowed to move until you do. Your fingers should be curled in except for your thumb and first finger, which will act like a pair of pincers.

4 As the right hand descends, open it fully so that the hidden coin is brought down on to the spectator's fingertips. The force of this motion will bounce the coin in their palm up in the air.

5 Grab the coin as it bounces, and the spectator will close their hand around the second coin. This occurs so fast it that is impossible for them to feel or see what has happened.

6 The spectator will think you failed, but when they open their hand, they will see that you have switched the coin!

tip *This is a genuine act of sleight of hand, which relies on fast movement and precision timing. With practice you will be able to perform it successfully nearly every time, but it doesn't matter if it takes more than one attempt, because it is not a trick but an example of your dexterity. In order to build a little routine, begin by simply taking the spectator's coin, without performing the switch. It is not as difficult as you might think. Explain that you want to try again and repeat it. The third time, execute the switch.*

coin through table

This quick trick will catch people off guard. A coin is made to pass straight through the centre of a table. Once you understand the *workings of the trick, try using three or four coins and making each coin pass through the table using a different method.*

1 With your left hand, tap a coin on the surface of a table at random points, explaining that every table has a particular "soft spot". Display the coin in your left hand in readiness for a Fake Take.

2 Now execute the Fake Take. With your right hand, pretend to pick up the coin. In reality the coin never moves from the left hand.

3 The right hand moves away, pretending to hold the coin in the fingertips. At the same time, the left hand drops below the table to a position directly under the right hand.

4 Slap the right hand flat on the table, and just at the same moment slap the coin on the underside of the table with your left hand. The result will be a sound which will make the spectators believe that the coin is under your right hand.

5 Pause for a few seconds and then slowly lift your right hand to show that the coin is no longer there.

6 Bring the coin out from below the table on the outstretched palm of your left hand.

coin through handkerchief

A coin is placed under the centre of a silk handkerchief. A layer of silk is lifted to confirm to the audience that the coin really is

underneath. Very slowly the coin begins to melt visibly through the fabric. The silk is unfolded to show the absence of any holes.

secret view

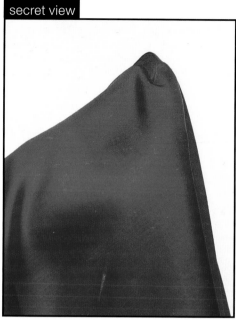

1 Hold a silk handkerchief by its edge in the left hand and display a coin in the fingertips of the right hand.

2 Drape the silk over the coin, positioning it directly in the centre, as shown here.

3 With the aid of your left hand, obtain a pinch of cloth between the back of the coin and your right thumb.

4 Lift the silk with your left hand to display the coin still held by the fingertips. Note how it is lifted back directly over the arm and above the other half of the silk.

5 Let go with your left hand and flick your wrist down so that both layers of the silk fall forward over the coin. The coin is now outside the silk, hidden under the pinch held by your thumb.

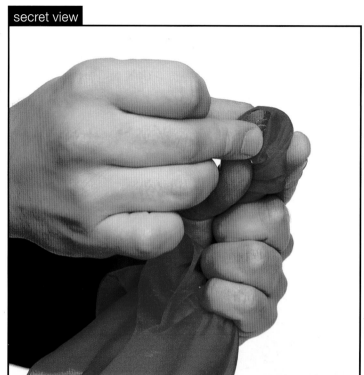

6 Wrap and twist the silk so that the shape of the coin is clearly visible through the fabric. Be careful not to expose the coin accidentally.

7 In this view from behind, you can see that the coin is being held by the fingers and the fabric that surrounds it. Begin to pull the coin up and into view.

8 From the front, the coin appears to be slowly melting through the silk. With practice, you will be able to make the coin look as if it penetrates on its own by simply pinching your left fingers together and using your right hand to support the coin as it emerges.

9 Remove the coin completely. Display both the coin and the silk – you can safely hand them to the audience for examination.

coin in egg

This is one of the many methods that exist for producing a coin from nowhere. These can either be used independently, perhaps to introduce a coin that you will proceed to use in another trick, or can follow on from a "disappearing" trick, to make a coin reappear.

In this trick, the mystery is increased by vanishing a marked coin borrowed from a spectator. The marked coin is then found inside an egg chosen at random by the spectator. With a little thought, there are many other places that you can make the coin appear from.

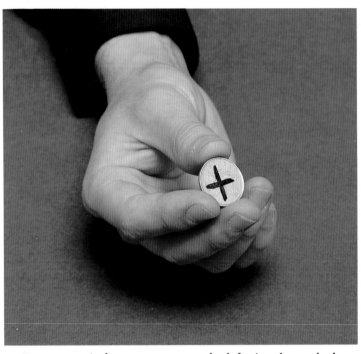

1 Borrow a coin from a spectator and ask for it to be marked with a permanent marker pen for later identification.

2 Vanish the coin using any of the methods described earlier. The coin should end up in Finger Palm position. The Coin Wrap would work well here.

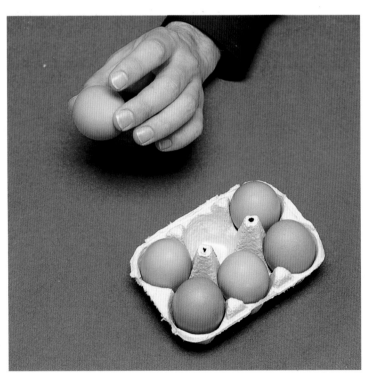

3 Display a box of eggs and ask someone to point to any one at random. Lift and display the egg with your left hand.

4 Transfer the egg to the right hand, placing it directly on top of the finger-palmed coin. The coin should remain completely hidden from view.

5 The left hand brings a glass to the centre of the table and the right hand taps the egg on the side of the glass, breaking the shell. The eggshell is opened with one hand so that the contents of the egg fall into the glass. Simultaneously allow the finger-palmed coin to drop into the glass with the egg. If timed correctly, it looks just as if the coin falls from the centre of the egg.

6 Scoop the coin from the glass with a spoon and have the mark verified as that which the spectator made a few minutes before. Have a napkin ready to wipe the coin dry. Using a similar method, you could also make the coin appear inside other impossible places, such an unopened can of food held by a spectator throughout the trick. The possibilities are endless.

coin in bread roll

In this trick, after "vanishing" a coin, you find it seconds later inside a bread roll that has been sitting on the table the entire time! To make this effect more astonishing, ask someone to mark the coin with a pen so that when they see it again they can be sure that it is the same coin. You could also ask them to choose from a selection of rolls, adding an extra dimension of mystery to the presentation.

secret view

1 Make a coin disappear, using one of the methods described earlier. Finish with the coin secretly hidden in your right hand. Ask someone to pass you a bread roll. Hold it with both hands so that the coin is hidden on the bottom. This view shows the right hand a split second before the roll is placed on top of the coin.

2 Bend both sides of the roll up so that the bottom splits open. With your fingers, begin to push the coin into the split. This exposed view shows the coin entering the roll. In performance, the bottom of the roll must be pointing down towards the table to hide these actions.

3 Bend the roll in the opposite direction with both hands so that the top cracks open. As it does so, the split at the bottom closes up and the coin appears to come from the centre! Ask the spectator to remove the marked coin and verify that it was the one they marked a few moments earlier.

coin through pocket

A coin is held against the outside of the trouser pocket and caused to pass through the fabric into the pocket! This quick routine makes use of the Finger Palm. It is quite easy to perfect and makes a good impromptu trick to remember for those times when you are stuck without props. Try to enhance the illusion by using the biggest, shiniest coin you can find.

1 Display a coin held against your right thigh, in line with the bottom of your pocket.

2 With both hands, pinch the fabric underneath the coin. Turn over the coin, simultaneously covering it from view with the fabric.

secret view

3 Secretly slip the coin into the right-hand Finger Palm position, using your thumb. This is unseen from the front. The photograph here shows your view.

4 With the coin still hidden in the Finger Palm, hold on to the top of the fold with your right first finger. Position your left first finger and thumb under the right and pinch a small piece of fabric.

5 Pull the fabric flat and show that the coin has vanished.

6 Reach into your right trouser pocket. Remove your hand with the coin displayed clearly at its fingertips.

bending coin (version 2)

Earlier in the book, Bending Coin (Version 1) showed how to create the illusion of a coin bending. You will now have learnt the necessary skill to perform a similar type of illusion, which is *the perfect follow-up. The amazing thing about this trick is that at the end you give the lender their coin back in its bent condition – a souvenir they can keep forever!*

secret view

1 To prepare, you need to bend a coin. First cover it with a cloth so that you do not mark it. Use a pair of pliers to hold the coin, then bend it with another pair of pliers. The result will be a coin that looks like the one shown here.

2 Before you begin, hide the bent coin in the right-hand Finger Palm position. Begin the performance by borrowing a coin which matches yours, and hold it in your fingertips as shown. Perform Bending Coin (Version 1) as described earlier.

3 At the end, hold your left hand out flat with the coin held in the right fingertips. You now apparently toss the coin from your right hand into the left. In reality, you perform the Bobo Switch, as described earlier.

secret view

4 This exposed view shows the bent coin lying on your left hand and the right coin about to be placed in the Finger Palm position. There should be no hesitation in your actions.

5 As the coin touches the left hand, it closes immediately into a fist so that the bend remains hidden. Squeeze the coin hard as if you are squashing it.

6 Open your left fingers wide to show that the coin really does have a bend in it. Give it back to the spectator, who will treasure the curiosity and think about it long after the event. As mentioned earlier, Bending Coin (Version 1) is a great prelude to this trick, and together they make a nice, memorable routine.

appearing money

Imagine reaching up into the air and producing real money. You would never have to work again! Your audience doesn't have to know the money was yours to start with. This is one of the best impromptu tricks you can perform. If you set up the trick prior to receiving your bill or check at the end of a meal, you can magically produce a tip for your waiter.

1 To perform this trick, you will need to wear a long-sleeved shirt. Take a banknote and fold it in half, widthways, down the middle.

2 Carefully roll the note tightly into a cigarette shape, starting at the fold, as shown here.

3 Place the rolled-up note into the crook of your left elbow. Fold over the fabric to hide the note and to keep it in place. Keep your arm bent to prevent the note from falling out.

4 Show your right hand empty, simultaneously pulling your sleeve up with your left hand. This should look very natural, and will make your audience less suspicious when you repeat it.

5 Repeat the motion with your left hand. However, as the right hand tugs the sleeve, it secretly grasps the rolled-up note from the crook of your elbow.

6 The exposed view shows how the left hand creates enough misdirection for this to happen. The right hand secretly retrieves the note, while the audience are focused on making sure that your left hand is empty.

7 Bring both hands to a position in front of you, at about chest level. The rolled-up note is held hidden in the right hand. The top end is pinched between the thumb, first and second fingers. These fingers pull the rest of the note back and out of sight.

8 From the front, both hands still look completely empty. This is a very convincing illusion.

9 Bring your fingers together and, without pausing, use your right thumb to pivot the note into a position that allows both hands to grip an edge each.

paper to money

A piece of blank, white paper is shown on both sides. It is folded several times and then unfolded again. It instantly changes into a banknote! The larger the value of the note, the more impressive the effect is. Try this out and you won't be disappointed. The success of the trick depends on the gimmick being made perfectly so that it operates easily and smoothly.

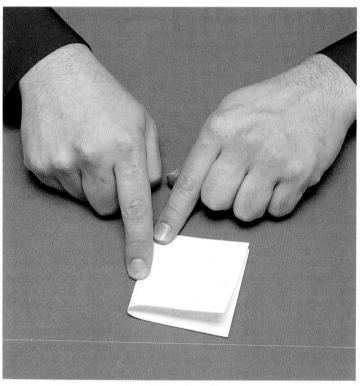

1 To prepare, cut a piece of paper exactly the same size as the banknote. Fold it neatly in half precisely down the middle.

2 Unfold the paper, turn it over and fold each side in half again, creasing the paper sharply and neatly.

3 Fold the paper along the creases, concertina-style, ensuring that the ends of the paper are to your right. Fold it up and towards you, making one final sharp crease directly down the centre.

4 Unfold the paper and repeat exactly the same procedure with the banknote. It is vital to the success of this trick that the creasing and folding is as neat and accurate as possible.

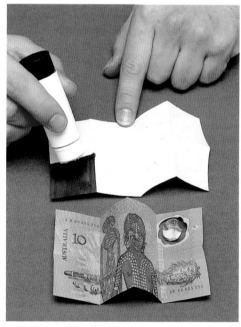

5 Apply glue to the upper right corner of the paper. (This section is marked in black for ease of explanation.)

6 Attach the glued corner of the paper behind the lower right corner of the banknote. Check that the edges match up exactly and that both pieces are perfectly aligned. Check the photograph here to ensure that you have orientated the papers correctly.

7 Fold the banknote along its creases so that you finish with it folded neatly at the top right corner of the white paper. If the edges of the banknote extend beyond the edges of the paper, the handling will be hindered.

8 Turn over the paper and hold it so that your right fingers cover the banknote, which is now positioned under the bottom right corner of the paper. This is how you should hold the paper when you begin the performance. The gimmick can be kept in a wallet or pocket until needed.

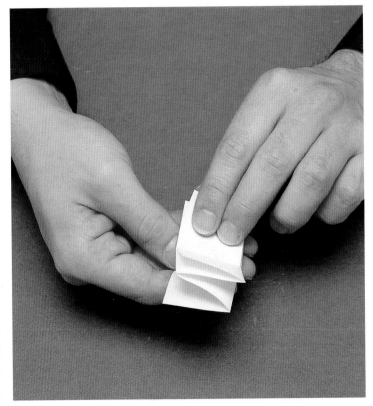

9 In performance, hold the paper with both hands, thumbs on top, fingers below. Quickly display the paper front and back by turning both wrists. When the back is seen, the banknote is hidden under the right fingers. Explain that money is printed on very special paper and that you have managed to find a piece.

10 With the front of the paper facing up once more, begin to fold the paper from left to right concertina-style, along the creases, with your left fingers. ▶

11 Fold the paper back towards you, still using the creases made previously. (Notice how the right hand stays in the same position throughout.)

12 Lift the right thumb and clip the package between the thumb and first finger. Then quickly lift the right third finger, clipping the paper between the right third and second fingers.

13 Squeeze these fingers together, flipping the package up at right angles to the fingers.

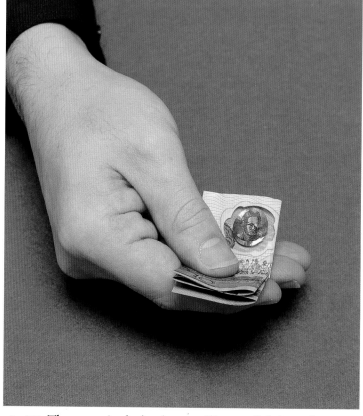

14 Your right thumb helps to turn the paper end over end. These steps are all done in one quick movement with a shake of the wrist, and take only a second.

15 The crease in the banknote will open slightly under its own tension. This enables the right thumb to push open the first fold without fumbling.

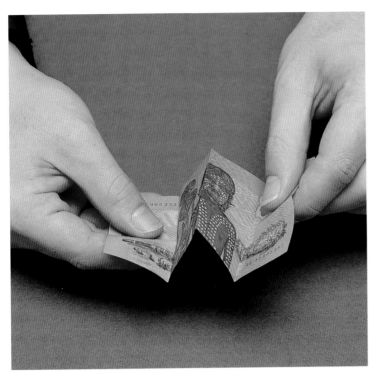

16 Immediately, the left fingers open the banknote out completely flat.

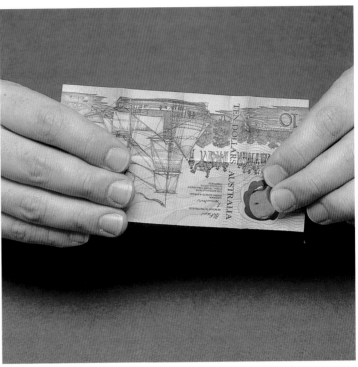

17 Turn your wrists, showing the back of the note exactly as you did at the start of the routine. This time it is the paper that is hidden under the right fingers.

18 Finish by displaying the front of the banknote again, then quickly put it away in your pocket or wallet.

tip *Make sure that you have a duplicate banknote (with similar crease lines) in your pocket or wallet so that if somebody asks to examine it, you can give them the duplicate note instead.*

glossary

There are many specialist words used within the magic fraternity, and their meanings may not be immediately obvious to a novice. The meanings of some of the most common terms are explained here.

Book test
A word or words chosen at random from a book which are revealed by the magician either as a prediction or through thought transference.

C & R
Abbreviated term for Cut and Restored. Often known as T & R (Torn and Restored).

Cabaret magic
A stand-up act, generally viewed from at least three sides and for a large crowd of people.

Close-up magic
The performance of magic shown very close to the audience, often using small everyday items.

Ditch
The secret disposal of an unwanted gimmick or object.

Fake (often spelt feke)
A secret piece of equipment. Same as a "gimmick".

Above: A sugar cube in the Classic Palm position.

Force
The action of influencing a spectator's choice. The spectator believes that their choice was fair.

Gimmick
Sometimes known as a "fake". A secret tool employed, often unseen, to cause the trick to work.

Illusion
Generally refers to large-scale magic tricks designed for a large audience.

Lapping
A technique used to secretly ditch objects in the lap. Always performed at a table and often used as a method for the disappearance of an object.

Levitation
An illusion which defies all known laws of gravity: the object or person seems to float with no visible means of support.

Manipulation
Any form of manual skill, but usually associated with the highly skilful performance of sleight of hand on stage, such as the production of coins.

Mentalist
The name given to a performer who specializes in mind-reading and other psychic effects.

Method
The secret workings of a trick.

Misdirection
The skill of focusing the minds or eyes of the audience on a particular point while secretly doing something else.

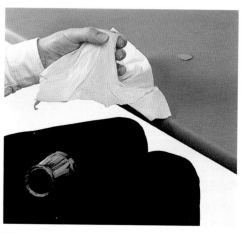

Above: Lapping a glass to make it disappear.

Optical illusion
An image that is distorted to create an untrue picture of what is being viewed, thus deceiving the eye. The impossibility of the optical illusion leads people to disbelieve or misinterpret what their eyes are showing them.

Palming
The secretion of an object in the hand. There are several different palms (Back Palm, Classic Palm, Finger Palm, etc). They do not necessarily use the palm of the hand itself.

Patter
The banter that accompanies the performance of a trick. This is a very important aid to "misdirection".

Penetration
The seemingly impossible action of a solid object passing through another.

Practice
The rehearsal required to make a performance appear slick and without mistakes.

Presentation
The overall term describing the trick, patter and style given to a routine.

Production
The magical appearance of an object.

Props

All the objects required for a particular effect to happen.

Routine

One whole trick or a series of tricks which lead from one to another.

Set-up

Preparation and often pre-arranged order of objects often – but not always – achieved secretly before the performance begins.

Silk

A piece of silk, or a silk handkerchief, fine enough to be folded and squeezed into a small space and thus easily hidden. Silks come in all shapes, sizes and colours.

Sleeving

The secret action of hiding an object in the sleeve.

Sleight of hand

The secret manipulation of an object. Often associated with close-up magic, but also very relevant to larger acts.

Stage magic

An act performed on stage for a large audience, often using large props and illusions. Similar to cabaret magic, which was a development of stage magic after the closure of many music halls and theatres at the end of the vaudeville era.

Stooge

A secret confederate in the audience who helps to make the magic happen.

Sucker trick

An effect that seems to let the audience in on the secret and then turns the tables at the last second. Also refers to a trick that appears to have gone wrong but is later proved to be part of the routine.

Suspension

Similar to levitation but describes the impossible balance of an object rather than a complete flotation.

T & R

Abbreviated term for Torn and Restored, often known as C & R (Cut and Restored).

Time misdirection

The term given to the technique of leaving time in between a secret move and the subsequent moment of magic. It is an additional way to hide the method to a trick.

Transformation

The term used to describe one object magically changing into another.

Transposition

Two or more objects which magically change places.

Vanish

To make an object disappear.

Above: The set-up for a T & R trick with napkins.

acknowledgements

The author would like to thank the following (past and present), who assisted in the process of writing this book: Aaron Barrie, Milbourne Christopher, Davenports, Edwin A. Dawes, Joanne Einhorn, John Fisher, Walter Gibson, Ian Keeble, George Kovari, Peter Laine, The Magic Circle and Christopher Pratt.

Thank you to the following, who provided props for photography: Ann Childers (money), Betty Davenport (antique box of tricks), Tim Ellerby (antique books), Jennifer Schofield (ring, money), Sarah See (money) and Amanda Wood (napkins, money).

Picture credits

suppliers

There are hundreds of magic shops all over the world that you may wish to visit in person or on the Internet. If your area is not listed below, take a look in your local business directory. Please note that the following details are correct at the time of publication, but it is advised that you contact the shops prior to your visit in order to avoid disappointment.

Australia
Bernard's Magic Shop
211 Elizabeth Street
Melbourne, Victoria
www.bernardsmagic.com.au

Hey-Presto Magic
Shop P34, Imperial Arcade
Pitt Street Mall
Sydney, New South Wales
www.hey-presto.com.au

Taylor's Magic Shop
Shop 1, The Interchange
432 Victoria Ave
Chatswood, New South Wales
www.taylorsmagicshop.com.au

Belgium
Mephisto Magic
(The Magic Hands)
Brugsesteenweg 166b
B-8520 Kuurne

Select Magic
CV Slachthuisstraat 21 8500
Kortrijk

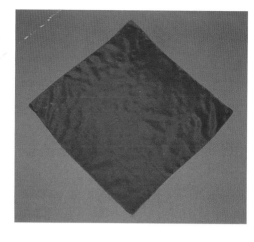

Canada
Browsers Den Of Magic
875 Eglinton Ave. W. #10
Toronto
www.browsersden.com

Magie Spectram Magic
1592 Jean-Talon est
Montréal
www.spectram.com

Morrissey Magic
2477 Dufferin Street
Toronto
www.morrisseymagic.com

Le Palais de la Magie
312 St-André Street
Gatineau
Québec
www.palaisdelamagie.com

Tony's Trick & Joke Shop
688 Broughton Street
Victoria
www.magictrick.com

Denmark
A & Z Magic
Ålekistevej 203 (basement)
2720 Vanløse
azmagic.net

France
Magic Productions
1 rue Froment, 75011
Paris

Mayette Magie Moderne
8 rue des Carmes, 75005
Paris
www.mayette.com

Germany
Astor Magie-Studio
Postfach 220 121D-42371
Wuppertal

Freer's Zauberladen
Greifswalder Str. 197
10405 Berlin

India
Electro Fun
9E Sandel Street, Calcutta 700016
www.electrofunmagic.com

Italy
La Porta Magica
Viale Etiopia 18, 00199
Roma
www.laportamagica.it

Japan
Magic Land
Tokyo
www.magicland-jp.com/Home/
LandMap.html

The Netherlands
Arjan's Show-Biz Centre
Bogerd 25
2922 EA Krimpen a/d Yssel
(By appointment only)
www.show-bizcentre.com

Dynamite Magic
Akkerwinde 7
5941 JP Velden
(By appointment only)
www.dynamitemagic.nl

Jan Monnikendam
Gedempte Raamgracht 5-7-9, 2011
WE Haarlem
www.monnikendam.nl

Spain
Magia Cadabra
Calle Navarros 7
Seville
www.magiacadabra.com

El Ray De La Magia
Calle Princesa 11
Barcelona

Selecciones Magicas
Calle Enamorandos 124
Barcelona

Switzerland
ZauberLaden Zürich
Hoerbi Kull
Rieterstr. 102
CH 8002
Zürich
www.zauberladen.com

Thailand
A & Z Magic
To find your nearest stockist, visit:
azmagic.net

UK
Davenports
7 Charing Cross Underground Arcade
The Strand, London
WC2N 4HZ
www.davenportsmagic.co.uk

International Magic
89 Clerkenwell Road
London
EC1R 5BX
www.internationalmagic.com

J.B. Magic
226 Lytham Road
Blackpool
Lancashire
FY1 6EX
www.jokeboxmagic.co.uk

Kaymar Magic
189a St Mary's Lane
Upminster
Essex
RM14 3BU
www.kaymarmagic.co.uk

USA
Abracadabra Magic
125 Lincoln Blvd
Middlesex, NJ
www.abra4magic.com

Daytona Magic
136 South Beach Street
Daytona Beach, FL
www.daytonamagic.com

Denny & Lee Magic Studio
325 South Marlyn Avenue
Baltimore, MD
www.dennymagic.com

Hank Lee's Magic Factory
112 South Street
Boston, MA
www.magicfact.com

Hocus Pocus
2311 E. McKinley
Fresno, CA
www.hocus-pocus.com

Hollywood Magic Inc
6614 Hollywood Blvd
Hollywood, CA
www.hollywoodmagicshop.com

Houdini's Magic Shops
Las Vegas, NV
www.houdini.com

Louis Tannen Inc
24 West 25th Street, 2nd Floor
New York, NY
www.tannenmagic.com

Stevens Magic Emporium
2520 E. Douglas
Wichita, KS
www.stevensmagic.com

Worldwide
Marvin's Magic
www.marvinsmagic.com

index